AFRICAN-CARIBBEAN
COMMUNITY ORGANISATIONS

The search for individual and group indentity

AFRICAN-CARIBBEAN COMMUNITY ORGANISATIONS

The search for individual and group indentity

Carl Hylton

Trentham Books

First published in 1999 by Trentham Books Limited

Trentham Books Limited
Westview House
734 London Road
Oakhill
Stoke on Trent
Staffordshire
England ST4 5NP

British Cataloguing in Publication Data
A catalogue record for this book is available from the
British Library
ISBN 1 85856 156 6

Cover painting by Ken Brown a Leeds-based artist.

Designed and typeset by Trentham Print Design Ltd., Chester and
printed in Great Britain by Professional Books Supplies Ltd, Oxford

Contents

Foreword

One of the great pioneers of Black self-improvement, Marcus Garvey, made it his life work to attack the very premise of colonialism. His movement was an assault upon the madness that left Black people a little less than human. So whether it is in the area of language or religion, of family structures or artistic manifestations, of political systems or economic processes of production, distribution and exchange, Africa's offspring have long been deemed incapable of advancing humanity unless with the civilising assistance of Europe. It is this fundamental canon of Western thought and ideology (whether of right, centre or left) that Garvey spent a lifetime challenging.

It is in the Garvey tradition that Carl Hylton has given his fascinating 'unpacking' of African-Caribbean community organisations. The book, as he himself says, 'documents the extent of the barriers individuals have to overcome in order to establish African-Caribbean group actions. The main external barriers to African-Caribbean group formation are racism and various forms of social exclusion, and the main internal barriers are age differentials, the control of group aims, gender divisions and parochial behaviour.'

Dr Hylton takes on the structural issues that make it difficult for Black organisations to either flourish or diminish. Hylton is careful not to give us a perspective that sees these organisations as a homogenous mass. Each has its own characteristics and micro-politics. But they share a number of common features, crucially, in that they seek an alternative to the dominant Euro-centric identity and also that there is a genuine engagement in the difficult notion of creating self-identity. This can be problematic given the 'different' agendas of external funders and the internal politics of the organisation.

I was surprised to discover just how many groups existed within a small area in Leeds (Chapeltown and Harehills). What did not surprise me was the dominance of arts groups. This again is characteristic of the Garvey tradition. In the keen struggle against 'mental slavery' we find that the frontline soldiers are the artists. This not to say that somehow Black people are not able in the area of business. Those frontline troops are needed to 'open' up possibilities and liberate the mind from the negative forces which seek to keep Black people limited and poor. What the creative artists have above all is 'vision' which is generated by the imagination. The problem for the politician, business person or even Community activist, is how to harness this same energy into their enterprise.

Hylton has shown that racism and internal politics have often been a hurdle too far for many Black organisations, who then combust under the pressure. Indeed, Garvey's own group was to decline as fast as it rose through a combination of mismanagement and a conspiracy amongst the white elite.

There are fundamental lessons here for any self-help group or individual. There is the real tension between the political desire to uplift your people and the 'pragmatics' of making a profit or getting funding. Hylton points us into another direction which perhaps breaks from this crude tension. He talks about the symbolic impact of many of these groups ñ in that their very existence provides psychological health to their members and those they serve. This is what can be called a symbolic assault on the ruling power structure. The Stephen Lawrence campaigners made much of positioning Stephen Lawrence's murder right at the core of the consciousness of middle England. They lacked funds, power and influence. However they did have a moral authority which eventually would shake the nation. Sadly, the official report metaphorically slipped out of the hands of grassroots Black organisations and the Lawrence report feels like someone is doing unto us, rather than capturing the range of black voices.

Hylton ends on a positive note and suggests that there is a symbiotic relationship between group formation and Black self-identity. The 21st century will demand that we all re-think our place in regard to nation, race, ethnicity, gender and class. As the pack gets shuffled it is important that Black people understand the implications of community groups as a vital framework for the preserving and the making of a range of Black identities.

Dr Tony Sewell, University Of Leeds

Acknowledgements

While most of the process of producing a work of this type demands many hours of lonely creativity, many people have directly and indirectly aided me during the past six years. I would first like to thank all the African, African-Caribbean and South Asian people interviewed formally in Leeds and London. Because of my direct involvement in African-Caribbean community groups in Leeds many 'grass-roots' activists such as Paul Auber, Val Blake, Kofi Nyaako, Annette Liburd and Joe Williams have also influenced my ideas. These rank-and-file activists are the key factors behind my spiritual, physical and intellectual survival. Credit should be given to my colleagues at the National Stepfamily Association (Angelle Bryan and Erica De'Ath), Exploring Parenthood (Lynthia Grant and Carolyn Douglas), the Institute of Community Studies (Geoff Dench), and the 'Race' and Public Policy Research Unit (RAPP) at the University of Leeds (Malcolm Harrison, Alan Deacon and Ian Law).

This work arises from my doctoral thesis, 'African-Caribbean Community Self Organisations: A Leeds Case Study', submitted to the Department of Sociology and Social Policy, University of Leeds in October 1997. My colleagues Alyas Karmani and Mark Priestley helped to sustain me with their philosophical discussions and practical assistance with computing issues. Kirk Mann provided academic and 'down to earth' wit, and my supervisor Ian Law gave crucial support in his laid-back style. The comments of examiners Harry Goulbourne and Colin Barnes improved the work, and the Department of Sociology and Social Policy provided financial assistance.

During the final phase of this work several people gave me valuable assistance. Paul Auber donated his reflective prose, 'The Maturing Activist', Ken Brown created the front cover painting, and Tony Sewell offered critical advice and wrote the foreword. But undoubtedly, without the support and commitment of Gillian Klein of Trentham Books this study might have been restricted to an academic elite – I am grateful.

To Ivan, Lela and the rest of my immediate and extended diasporian family.

Reflective prose:
The Maturing Activist

... The very essence of the activist is to provide activity in a given, or series of given situations, using the intuition, skills and knowledge that have been available to, and compelled the activist toward activism since time in memorial! This is an age-old and lonely work, despite creature comforts or vested power. Yet, for those who embrace it, the harvest is great!

More often than not, as in the times of our fathers and their fathers before them, the maturing activist – unaware of the nature or the compelling power of his or her activism – find themselves isolated in a state of personal frustration and despair! Beware! For this purgatorial state of limbo is peopled with the vitriolic djinn of Bitterness and Cruelty, ever on the watch to fuel a jealousy of those peers who, in thy regard, and despite the quality of their input, or indeed, whether they input at all, seem to constantly, and materially, and vaingloriously benefit!

Suffice to say why – for the fruit of their labours is for future understanding. There is no satisfaction to be gained for an activist dwelling on the anticipation of pecuniary advantage in activism. To do so is to create stumbling blocks and obstacles to activistic maturity, and to weave false illusions for oneself, and ultimately for those whom ye serve. For the activist, personal profit can only give satisfaction if it is the declared and primary objective of the activity. Since the course of the bulk of the true activist's work is socially oriented, activity for personal profit can have its contradictions. Be aware of these!

However, this is not to say the activist must go about hungry. On the contrary, together with applying purpose and integrity to work, the activist must cultivate a capacity for delayed gratification, in the spirit of that 'table being prepared in the presence of those real or imagined enemies'! The activist open to the satisfaction contained in the result of work – oftentimes invisible to the non-activist – is always open to the pecuniary or otherwise rewards of their genuine activism. What is more, the activist is able to see and receive reward, to 'sit, and be anointed and to eat' whether in public or private. After all, is this not part of the promise?

The invisible results of work provide their own rewards in the portion of the harvest, in fruits which can never be eaten by the non-activist! It is as much an act of faith as it is a fact of logic, and when understood by the activist, the portion assigned is found to be edible and uncontentious.

I tell you these things to encourage you and to arm you, for the maturing activist must be vigilant if he or she would dispel the bitterness and the cruelty of professional jealousy, and thereby attain activistic maturity! ...

From – 'The Activist's Bible Companion'
Paul Auber
Leeds, 1998

Note
Bible texts – Psalm 23: 5, Ephesians 6: 10-18 and St. Luke 10: 2-12.

Introduction

Although the importance of community organisations is recognised as a feature of African-Caribbean life in the UK, details about the difficulties of building and sustaining group activity have not been adequately recorded. Better understanding of the links between the creation of individual and group identity is also needed. This book provides an analysis of the struggles for individual and community self-consciousness or identity which can be transposed to any city with a significant population of people of African descent. There is a counter position between the individual and the group. Using postmodernist approaches, the arguments express an African-Caribbean fight for the right to define the methods and outcomes of their individual participation in UK society (self-autonomy) which presupposes a direct link with African-Caribbean group autonomy.

Racism and social exclusion are key factors influencing the reactions of African-Caribbean activists. They are excluded from many existing voluntary and statutory organisations because the services available do not adequately meet their needs (Hylton, 1995; Law, Hylton, Karmani and Deacon, 1994). Group actions are initiated to counter the effects of racism and various forms of social exclusion from such key areas of UK society as education, health care and employment. But although group actions help to alter specific practical difficulties they also help to create a positive sense of individual and collective identity which is linked to African and Caribbean ideals. African names and African concepts are used, and western ideas, actions and interpretations of history which exclude African knowledge are questioned. Not only do individuals have to overcome the external barriers of racism and social exclusion, but they also have to deal with internal barriers to group formation. In this study the three most significant internal barriers are age differentials, gender divisions, and the differences linked to place of birth and locality.

The term African-Caribbean refers to individuals of African descent who were born in the Caribbean or the UK but who can trace their ancestral lineage to Africa via parents who were born in the Caribbean. In Leeds the majority of African-Caribbeans involved in community organisations were born in either the UK or on the Caribbean islands of Jamaica, Barbados or St. Kitts and Nevis. A few were born on the continent of Africa in countries of the west coast such as Ghana and Nigeria, and they are included and differentiated as the need arises. In many cases they are key players in organisations with majority African-Caribbean focus and clientele. The African activists are interesting because they have worked to overcome the gulf that in practice tends to separate the two communities: African-Caribbeans and continent-born Africans. Although there is a strong wish at the philosophical and practical levels, especially among members of the African-Caribbean community, to come to terms with their African heritage using the knowledge as a spring-board for present and future actions against the racism of UK society, there still exists a gulf between the two groups of people. This tends to work at the level of internalising negative stereotypes of each other, with African-Caribbeans blaming continental Africans for assisting their transportation into slavery. Tensions also exist between women and men of African-Caribbean descent linked to the widening socio-economic gap between them and the differential treatment in UK society, where males are alienated and women viewed as icons. This has resulted in an ongoing community debate concerning the roles of women and men, the family, the African-Caribbean community, and the prospects for positive survival strategies for the future. These gender issues are explored in Chapter 3.

This study is in the tradition of ethnographic or anthropological research of the Chicago School or the work of Alaine Tourraine in analysing social movements pressure groups. Similar themes can be found in the approach adopted by Swedish researcher Ulf Hannerz (1969) in his exploration of African-American urban life, Geoff Dench's (1975) work on the Maltese in London, and David Robins (1992) analysis of disaffected inner city youths attached to a construction training workshop in London. These researchers tell the story of the actors from inside their world. Hannerz spent two years living just a few streets outside a predominantly African-American area in Washington. For four years Robins was instructor to, and confidant of inner city youths attending a construction training workshop.

Although these research approaches are informative they differ from the method adopted in this study in one major respect. I am an African-Caribbean researcher and community activist. I agree with Harry Goulbourne (1990) that there is an urgent need for African-Caribbeans to find their own academic voices. One outcome will be to shift the focus on African-Caribbeans as actors rather than as victims of racism. This study is a step along this path: by going beyond the approaches of researchers from the majority community the research presents a different style. The emphasis is similar to Paul Gilroy's early work (1987), *There Ain't no Black in the Union Jack* which had an edge, a spark, a fire of passion and truth, 'telling it as it is' in an effort to uplift people of African descent. His later works such as *Black Atlantic* (1993), although informative, could have been written by any Eurocentric researcher because of its cryptic content and a style devoid of reality and change potential for African actors. In contrast a recent small scale research study concerning African-Caribbean youths in Brixton entitled *This is where I live* (Haynes, 1996), and the Africancentric work of African-Canadian Wanda Bernard on the survival strategies of African-Canadian and African-Caribbean men in the UK, are reaffirmations of Gilroy's earlier work. Although not overtly Africancentric Goulbourne's work has the change potential of the African-Caribbean insider activist, illustrated most clearly in his introduction to *Black Politics in Britain*, where he agrees with Gordon Lewis (1983).

> We desperately need to include black people's own interpretations of their reality and the action they have taken to change or modify their situations. The failure of much British 'race relations' research and writing to move into this gear runs the danger of developing and cementing a tradition of scholarship in which, to paraphrase Gordon Lewis, we see victimization but not the victim, we see the forces of anti-racism, but not the anti-racist, we see the process of institutional change but not the groups and individuals who fight for such changes. (Goulbourne, 1990, 3)

He is not alone in this quest. On 28 October 1995 two hundred people attended a conference at Sheffield University entitled 'African Centred Research: A Way Forward'. Most were of African descent. They came because they were involved in research with African and African-Caribbean people or wanted to become involved. Both groups were unhappy with the existing 'race' relations research industry, dominated by European Eurocentric researchers who command research grants to work 'on' rather than 'with' their respondents. The conference was subtitled 'Making Our Own History', thus indicating the need for researchers of African descent to define the research agenda. This sentiment corresponded with the mood of the delegates who strongly articulated the view that people of African descent are not victims, and furthermore that research should be used as one among a range of strategies to empower African and African-Caribbean communities. These activists believe that research should provide a voice for the communities, putting into practice the notion of 'lift as we climb'.

Similar arguments concerning autonomy were expressed by one hundred men of African descent who attended a conference in May 1997 at the West Yorkshire Playhouse in Leeds. At this unique event, entitled 'Black Men in Britain: Marching into the Millennium', issues such as school exclusions, unemployment, petty crime and imprisonment, fatherhood responsibilities and lack of African-Caribbean male pro-activity in community groups were successfully discussed. One of the clearest points of agreement was the need for men of African descent to be in control of their destiny. They have to set the agenda about issues affecting their lives by discussion and leading actions, workshops and research and publication of results. Africans and African-Caribbeans should remain the experts on their own lives, family and community, and social policy makers should take their initiatives from this lead (Hylton [ed.], 1997). The contents of this book are a contribution to the project of Africans and African-Caribbeans making their own history.

Research locality

The main data was generated in the northern UK city of Leeds, two hundred miles from London. With representatives of seventy-five nationalities in the city, Leeds can be considered a multi-ethnic *area*, although the main ethnic groups – South Asians, African-Caribbeans and Africans are concentrated in a few inner city areas in the north east and north west of the city. The 1991 census indicates Leeds' total population as 680,722, with 22,536 South Asians including Pakistanis, Indians and Bangladeshis, 1,343 Africans, and 6,554 people of African-Caribbean descent. In 1967 Butterworth could report that half the immigrant population of Leeds including Africans, African-Caribbeans, South Asians, Yugoslavians, Poles and Russians lived in the former Jewish enclave of the city called Chapeltown. Fifty years ago this area was considered a white middle class stronghold, with its wide roads, large terraced houses and detached mansions. Chapeltown lies approximately three miles north east of the city centre on hills which guaranteed clean fresh air beyond the confines of the congested central industrial areas.

> The build-up of the Jewish population in Chapeltown began in the years immediately before 1914. An analysis of three typical streets in the area, from the Directory of 1900, showed one Jewish householder out of 146; the Directory of 1914 showed 36 Jewish householders, one of which was the Rabbi. The increase in the Jewish population continued between the wars, probably reaching its peak at the end of the war in 1945. After that, there was a rapid decline as movements to the suburbs acquired momentum and other groups, notably Poles and Eastern Europeans, moved in. The social character of the middle-class part changed rapidly: the houses in the area lent themselves to sub-letting, and immigrants and others moved in because housing was easier to get there than elsewhere. (Butterworth, 1967, 58)

Although Fryer (1991, 1) documents people of African descent in the UK from the third century AD, the contemporary settlement of African-Caribbeans in Leeds stems from the Second World War. Caribbean military personnel were based in Leeds at *'the Camp Road Barracks, which now forms part of the Little London Estate'*. Caribbean workers were also recruited for the industrial front. Men known as the 'Bevan Boys' worked as miners in Yorkshire pits and women worked in engineering at Kirkstall Forge or Blakeys, or in hospital services in Leeds. After the war twenty or thirty Caribbean servicemen settled in the Hyde Park area of Leeds. They were soon joined by others coming directly from the Caribbean to meet the labour shortage in the UK (Gallagher, 1992). A similar pattern of resettlement occurred in other industrial areas in the UK (Fryer, 1991; Ramdin, 1987).

The move to the Chapeltown area began in the late 1950s, coinciding with the withdrawal of Jewish inhabitants to Leeds outer suburbs such as Moortown. At present the African-Caribbean community in Leeds exceeds 10,000 people, with the majority concentrated in the inner city areas of Chapeltown and Harehills. Here the term community is used to denote a group of people with real or perceived feelings of common interests such as culture, ethnicity, religion or locality. Racism and social exclusion have sometimes been an important catalyst in the formation and retention by Africans, African-Caribbeans and South Asians of concepts concerned with separate communities. Similar to other regions of major African-Caribbean residency in the UK, the Leeds African-Caribbean population mirrors the historical patterns of pre and post war settlements, with continuing struggles against racism and unemployment. These factors can be gauged by the representatives of African-Caribbean organisations in the city. They have the remit of combating racism and sexism, the maintenance or re-establishment of cultural distinctiveness, religious worship, advice and advocacy work around housing, education, and social security benefit entitlement, mental health, drugs, the effects of contact with the police and the provision of supplementary education such as Saturday schools. To this list of organisational strategies can be added the individual and collective approaches to African and African-Caribbean art forms.

Similar organisations occur in other major inner city areas of African-Caribbean residence. So the African-Caribbean residents of Leeds provide a meaningful guide concerning the range of ideas and activities within the UK African-Caribbean community. It is no coincidence that in all major UK cities of African-Caribbean residence similar cultural, advocacy, education and social organisations can be found. For instance, if we consider another city outside London such as Leicester, which is multicultural and has a university and an African-Caribbean population of similar size, we find, as in Leeds, island associations, housing associations, sports associations including a Caribbean cricket club, a Carnival Committee, arts associations, business associations, community radio stations and provisions for elderly African-Caribbean citizens (Afrikan-Caribbean Support Group Research Project, 1992). This is not to deny that there are differences, such as the unique pioneering groups presently found in Leeds' African-Caribbean community. For instance, Frontline Self-Build Housing Association was the first Black self-build scheme in the north of England. Other pioneers include Kuffdem Arts, an innovative community theatre project, the Palace Youth Project, one of the longest running youth projects in the UK, and the Afrikan Curriculum Development Association who design and deliver pre-Access courses and have a formal partnership agreement with the University of Leeds.

Leeds' African-Caribbean community has a vibrancy of group activity, particularly in Chapeltown and Harehills where many who are involved form an inter-linked network and are actively engaged in several African-Caribbean organisations at once. The wider African-Caribbean community who use the services may or may not be actively involved in the day-to-day control and continuation strategies of the organisations. Though it might appear that the range and expertise of local African-Caribbean groups will be well known in the community, in reality there are many African-Caribbeans in Leeds who are unaware of the range of group activities. Also, those actors who are aware of the extent of local group activities may be unclear about the significance of all of them.

In trying to describe and analyse the significance of African-Caribbean group actions I aim to present data from fieldwork research in Leeds and London and to find methods of expressing why and how group activity occurs. I am not trying to force this data to conform to out-dated theories. The research outcome has to make sense to rational enquiry and, more importantly, the analysis has to make sense to the actors whose lives are being described and analysed. African-Caribbeans are experts in their own lives. My research training and academic credentials do not give me the right to create analytical frameworks which bear no relation to reality. I believe that the outcome of research involving visual minorities (Africans, African-Caribbeans and South Asians) has to be beneficial to them. It is their story told in an academic format. This study is situated in an academic tradition but the underlying theme is to undermine its power in an attempt to give credibility to the subjects of research. The outcome is xx • AFRICAN-CARIBBEAN COMMUNITY ORGANISATIONS

not to view actors as animals in a zoo or to test theoretical paradigms on a group of exotic characters for the benefit of academic debate. The priority is to make a faithful record of events in a manner useful not only for theorists but also for activists and the wider African-Caribbean community in the UK. In looking at the relationship between a non-disabled researcher and disabled people, Mark Priestley has constructed a useful model of 'coparticipatory' research methods where the people being researched share *control over aspects of the research production process, including the dissemination of research outputs'* (Priestley, 1998, 23), and this has influenced my approach.

Research methods

The majority of the fieldwork data was generated from African-Caribbean organisations based in Leeds. I used three methods of data gathering: (i) literature searches and content analysis of written materials such as pamphlets, leaflets, flyers, meeting notes and annual reports produced by the groups, (ii) semi-structured interviewing and (iii) participant observation. The operationalisation of these research methods can be further elaborated into three distinct stages.

Stage one entailed the compilation of an audit of the African-Caribbean organisations situated mainly or operating in Chapeltown and Harehills. These two districts contain 5,500 of the 10,000 African-Caribbean residents of Leeds.

Stage two involved producing a semi-structured interview schedule that would form the basis of individual interviews with key members of eleven African-Caribbean organisations purposely selected from the audit complied at stage one. The total number of ninety-three African-Caribbean self-organised groups were divided into twelve categories: advice and advocacy, arts, education, business and training, health advice and support, housing, religion, savings and finance, social, sport, women's support groups and others. Group activists were selected and interviewed to include, where possible, representatives of each category and how long the group had been operating, in an effort to create a balance between new and older groups. Other criteria were whether the group catered mainly for female or male clients, and whether the group or activist would yield significant data. Allied to these purposive selection procedures was my personal involvement and intimate knowledge of the groups and activists involved. At this juncture it would be useful to articulate some of the arguments used to clarify the notion of group self-organisation or self-activity used here.

Self-organisation or community control of the group's agenda and actions are of paramount importance to all grass-roots organisations. When control impedes African-Caribbean aspirations, passions can flare. The spectre of colonialism, exploitation, racism and slavery can readily be linked – correctly or not – to funding restriction issues. Self-organisation can be an indication that all or most group members have the same ethnicity and use funds generated by group members, rejecting 'outside' financial aid. This position is emphased by Rastafarians on Liverpool's *Frontline* where their leader 'Gaddafi' spoke about the renovation of a building for their use. This work was being undertaken without 'outside' financial aid.

> It's only at the age of thirty that I-man beginning to understand what Garvey stands for. Pride of the black man. You can't have pride if you are always begging. ... We doing an independent t'ing. I and I don't want no government handout. Too many strings attached. And I and I don't want no Babylonian telling I and I what to do. Seen Rasta? (Dennis, 1988, 35)

Financial aid could perhaps be taken from selected 'other' agencies such as those predominantly controlled by visual minority people. The question is whether community control can be exercised if financial and other assistance is taken from agencies who are 'ethically sound'. African-Caribbean organisations may have to consider further issues such as the type of controls placed on the group by funding agencies. Can these controls be negotiated and the group's aims remain intact? To achieve group self-organisation might entail having various partnership agreements distributed over several funding agencies, so that the group's survival can be maintained if one of the agreements fails. This can entail the withdrawal of funding or the imposition of new conditions undermining the group's autonomy. From this maze of variables I intend to use the concept of African-Caribbean self-organisations as a situation where there may be significant differences and tensions regarding activity and outlook between African-Caribbean groups whose major funders place some limitations on the group's activities, but where the group and community members define their own agenda. Some of these themes linked to cultural identity are explored in a recent conference publication from Liverpool edited by William Ackah and Mark Christian (1997).

Finally, *Stage three* involved the generation of further data by individual and group interviews in London and Leeds with voluntary and statutory family advice and support service providers and African-Caribbean group members such as Sokka Gakkai International (SGI), UK Buddhists, Rastafarians, Seventh Day Adventists and lone parents. Most of this work was conducted as an aspect of my involvement as a researcher in action research projects at the National Stepfamily Association, the Institute of Community Studies, Exploring Parenthood, and the 'Race' and Public Policy Research Unit (RAPP) at the University of Leeds.

Explaining individual and group activity is the very stuff of the social sciences, with the former falling into the psychological and the latter into the social. Most psychological explanations seek to determine activity as an individual cognitive process entailing minimal or negative cultural or group interference in the perception of such actions. In crude terms, the individual acts without reference to others, whether they are family, friends or share the same cultural group, class or socio-economic position. Group explanations fall into the orbit of sociology, seeking to account for actions by reference to the forces outside of the individual: 'social forces'. Here actions are viewed as a combination of 'outside' factors such as family, friends, cultural group, class or socio-economic position. These factors are included as a part of the cognitive and experiential map of actors, persuading them that others are situated in similar social positions to themselves. It is the belief that other individuals and groups are affected by the same or similar social forces which might be changed not solely by individual actions but by group activity. On the basis of research with twenty-six national organisations and twenty-four local self-help groups using semi-structured interviews, Wann (1995) concluded that:

> For individuals, joining a self help group is a means of ending social isolation, bringing people together who share a particular experience

or concern. Groups are a source of compassion, information and advice based on first-hand experience, and provide tangible help with practical difficulties.

... self help is about personal responsibility and interdependence, as well as direct, local action. Its ethos is empowering and enabling rather than protective, prescriptive or philanthropic.

Although aspects of this present study draw on philosophical, psychological and sociological disciplines it leans mainly towards the sociological and cites examples tested by practical experiences. So the theoretical is linked to the practical, allowing us to view, understand, and analyse African-Caribbean group actions. This approach is not only of academic interest but the outcomes may help to engender constructive change through critiques that make sense to the individuals and groups involved. Theories resisting conversion to practical activity may retain their perfection as idealist future forms while remaining incapable of affecting change to those forms. The majority of critical theory and post-modernism might be included under this umbrella, with the exceptions of Melucci, (1988 and 1989) Jamerson (1984 and 1985) and Marcuse (1972).

Individual and group relationship

In the western liberal tradition we are categorised as autonomous individuals who are atomised but self-assured. It is claimed that this self-assurance is nurtured in a nuclear two parent female and male family unit. Networks of friends and acquaintances are constructed from this base on the assumption that all individuals inevitably operate in a similar manner thus forming a huge chain of inter-linked individuals-families-friends-localities-counties-nation states. In this liberal middle class framework, successes and achievements are conducted through individual effort requiring patience, thrift and sheer hard work (McLennan, 1990). When individuals do not maintain this model relationship, particularly the notion of remaining atomised isolated beings, an explanation has to be found. Individuals begin to form groups – sometimes only for the purpose of pursing joint activities such as sports and recreation or various past-times that may be easier or more interesting if they occur in a communal environment. The explanations for the formation and continuance of these types of groups is not explored here, because my concern is the explanations and analyses for group activities that occur for cultural and political reasons. Such groupings occur for the purposes of maintaining or rebuilding cultural identities or to influence and change the political structures or climate of local and national events, particularly where structures and actions have a direct bearing on the lives of African-Caribbean people and their descendants now living in the UK. Nevertheless, not all sports and recreational type groups have been excluded because some of these groups have cultural implications as an aspect of their development and continuance, such as the maintenance of a particular cultural identity.

Although class position is a factor in their oppression, African-Caribbeans in Leeds view ethnicity as the major force impinging on their lives. Working class organisations such as trade unions and left-wing political parties do not have a major impact on their ideas and actions in community politics. African-Caribbean community self-organisations are a reflection of this situation: they build group activity for self-defence to retain self-respect by trying to rebuild an African culture that has been brutalised through the middle passage and survives only partially in the western diaspora. The organisations try to assist African-Caribbeans to compete on a more equal footing in a racist society, as exemplified in Leeds by the Palace Youth Project and Chapeltown Independent After School. African-Caribbean groups with specific universalisms proclaiming such notions as that all workers of the world are united, do not exist in Leeds. This does not imply that African-Caribbean groups do not extend their aspirations and actions beyond Leeds and the UK – some groups do have a wider outlook, for instance, the Black Women in Europe Network, which highlights the concerns of Black women in Europe. There are also very strong notions that all people of African descent are linked by their oppression in time, space and history. Such universalism is linked to the world's Black experience. What is important is that this linkage is not concerned with class because in a racist culture higher class status does not detract from personal oppression, although such oppression may be at a different level or focus. The lowly status of the group to which one belongs can never be completely overcome. According to Koval (1988, xci-xcii):

... for the black individual there is no escaping the whiteness of the society except by denying who he or she is – and that is no escape at all. It does not matter if he makes a million dollars a year for leaping high above a ten-foot basket; or accumulates many more millions by selling records; ... or even gets to sit on the board of directors of truly white corporations, ... he, or she, will still be defined by an other whose power and dominion are white. And in this order of blackness is Otherness.

It is with these notions that groups organise to defend, but they also try to raise their group as opposed to their individual status. Individual status becomes closely linked to group status, this being the status the group holds in a given society. By improving the status of the group to which you belong you also improve how you are viewed as an individual. Thus can the different strata in the African-Caribbean community act against their class interest (in the Marxist sense) and for the group interest. These arguments are opposed to the group action analysis by meta-theorists such as John Rex. He has utilised his fieldwork data to built a huge edifice of theoretical work to explain visual minority group action as an aspect of class action. He has tried to link the class action of Marx with the status of Weber. In 1983 he stated that his method of analysis was 'empirical class analysis' with the use of ideal types (Rex, 1983, 196). As part of an argument first made in 1986 and reiterated in 1991, Rex puts forward the notion of what he terms 'ethnic groups' operating as 'quasi-classes'. They are not separate classes but a part of the 'indigenous' working class with the capability of acting for their own interests with their own organisation to pursue a type of class struggle of their own (Rex, 1991, 114). Significantly, he is aware that African-Caribbean group actions cannot be explained only in terms of metropolitan class theory because much more is involved.

... a great deal of West Indian political activity is not only concerned simply with worker rights or even conflicts with the local police. It is very much concerned with finding ways of undoing the wrongs done by four hundred years of slavery. (Rex, 1991, 195)

Means and ends rationale

Another important feature of African-Caribbean group activity is the notion of means/end rationale. The phase 'the means are the ends', encapsulates why mainstream and left political groupings cannot incorporate the aspirations of the majority of African-Caribbeans in the UK. It is also why in Leeds, African-Caribbean groups are organised to achieve their goals through the living process of the means. How goals are to be achieved is as important, if not more so, as the goals themselves. The processes of change become a matter of self-pride and achievement. Actors are aware they are able to articulate and carry out their own or local agendas with the knowledge that local people have been involved in its creation and execution. Although not all group aims are deliberately geared to a socialist type strategy, many African-Caribbean groupings in Leeds and elsewhere will agree with Sivanandan (1990, 76) that:

> Any liberation struggle which is not socialist in the first instance ends up in tyranny. The means are the ends, there can be no distinction between them. There is no socialism after liberation, socialism is the process through which liberation is won.

Such changes are achieved through the process of self-organisation. An analogy can be made here with the recasting of the term black from a negative when applied to people of African descent, to a positive term during the 1950s and 1960s. Similarly, African-Caribbeans have aimed to recast their various forms of social exclusion from UK society in the 1970s, 1980s and 1990s into a positive with the aid of their community self-organisations and struggles for local autonomy. Whereas it might appear that African-Caribbeans are not, according to Goulbourne (1988), engaged in 'politics', it might be more correct to view African-Caribbean group and political involvement as another type of struggle that is also highly political, although such commitment and involvement are mainly separate from the mainstream democratic political party structures and Marxist groupings. The paraphrased words of Stafford Scott, leader of Broadwater Farm Youth Association is poignant here. Addressing a public meeting in Haringey Town Hall on 10 November 1985, he proclaimed that in today's struggles *'being political now requires complete disassociation from the corporate structures of formal politics which are in need of drastic re-politicization. Authentic politics is thought to recommence with this act of withdrawal'* (Gilroy, 1987, 228).

Many African-Caribbean organisations are aware of the dilemma of trying to create separate autonomy where there is a potential for funders to control group agendas. Some groups such as the Rastafarians on Liverpool's Front-line have refused this financial 'outside' aid in their endeavours to maintain an independence of action, spirit and pride (Dennis, 1988, 35). Other groups have had to try and establish various strategies so they can fulfil their goals with the minimum of interference from funding bodies, whether national or locally based. One example is the Leeds-based Afrikan Curriculum Development Association (ACDA), a project that has developed and delivered post-16 Afrikancentric courses to the local African-Caribbean community. Part of their control agenda entails having various partnership agreements with funding agencies such as the University of Leeds, Department of Adult and Continuing Education (Hylton, Blake, Auber, Kasule, Karisa and Kopoka, 1996).

Ethnicity

The final paradigm worthy of note relates to explanations involving ethnicity as a factor of organisational strategy. According to Wievioka (1992):

> ... 'ethnic movements' bear feelings of subjectivity, set up stakes in the cultural realm and try to affect the debate of ideas.

In the ethnicity paradigm the call to action is focused on the shared ethnic origins of group participants. This involves the affirmation of shared common origins, heritage and cultural identity. For African-Caribbeans such a call to activity presupposes a restatement of cultural and ethnic identity devalued by European culture. Activity revolves around a sense of belonging. According to Bacal (1991, 18) paraphrasing Stavenhagen (1984):

> ... allegiance to an ethnic community provides a sense of belonging and meaning as an intermediate level of relations between the individual and the bureaucratized political society, ... the revival of ethnic identity nowadays may be an adaptive response to the increasing alienation of individuals in mass society.

The Black consciousness movements of the 1960s and 1970s were built on an ethnic or cultural framework spear-headed by notions pertaining to 'Black power'. Consciousness demanded a review of self and group identity, casting doubts on the given notions of negativity attributed by society to people of African descent. Such self-help pro-jects created a rediscovery and renewed positive identity where a 'new' type of ethnicity could be affirmed, so creating a new sense of power – the power to take control of self-image, history, and thus create and re-establish the broken link with the past. Thus the individual and the African-Caribbean ethnic group used a new force, a power, a Black power for their own emancipation that was both spiritual and prac-tical. The key to such activity was and is an acceptance and celebra-tion of being Black, of being African. This constituted a positive ethnicity of being the 'other'.

The ethnicity paradigms as the sole determinate of African-Caribbean group activity might indeed provide some adequate descriptive models for Black conscious collective actions. However, this explanatory con-cept fails to explain the difficulties of building and sustaining actions undermined by tensions between actors from the same ethnic group-ings. Such difficulties are encountered between African-Caribbeans from different class positions, and also between 'new activists' and 'indigenous activists', female and male actors, and Africans born on the African continent and others born in the Caribbean or the UK. The indigenous activists are African-Caribbeans who were born in Leeds and are involved in African-Caribbean group organisations. They have direct experience of the negative outcomes from the pres-sures directed at the local African-Caribbean community. They have witnessed and helped to build and sustain many of the coping strategies utilised in the community, but they have also been powerless to counteract certain negative outcomes. These activists tend to offer theoretical and practical initiatives in which consolidation is a major theme and where actions are geared to the building of a strong bridge-head in the local area. Their arguments tend to follow a pattern: if we cannot extend elsewhere in the city, if living space, education and jobs are closed to us, then we lay claim to the urban space we are forced to occupy. Such spaces are fiercely defended.

The new activists are classified as African-Caribbean actors who have come to Leeds from other large UK cities or from the African conti-nent. They may have attained higher formal educational qualifications than some of the indigenous actors. These new activists have to cope with the fear of rejection by some of the local African-Caribbean community. Their input and ideas may not be accepted if their activities are seen as a threat to the ideas and working methods of local indigenous actors. Newcomers have to tread a thin line and build a climate of acceptance by indigenous actors and the local African-Caribbean community. Credibility is created by the long term assessment of 'good' deeds. This does not entirely reduce all antagonisms, although it may help to project the good intentions of the 'outsider'. New actors have to be aware of this type of blockage that can arise when they indulge in local group input – they have to be skilled and patient. In many instances during the early stages, new actors have to give in when their ideas and actions clash drastically with local accepted norms or the efforts of respected indigenous actors. Importantly also, 'outsiders' should not expect to receive praise or strong acknowledgements from indigenous actors and the wider African-Caribbean community for their input to the group. This is especially true during the first couple of years of group involvement. If new actors are not flexible enough, especially in the early stages, their actions can be misunderstood as 'out-of-tune' with the local African-Caribbean ethics. All new actors are at risk of this potential label. Africans with academic qualifications, who may have had limited contacts with African-Caribbeans, have to be especially careful.

The local African-Caribbean fear of 'outsiders' – even when the outsider shares the same ethnic origins as the community – stems partly from the community's real experiences of being 'used'. In the past this has taken the form of information being gathered about the community and then sometimes used for personal gain in a manner that did not advance the interests of the community. What is more, such data has been used without gaining prior consent from the individuals concerned. Another reason for cautiousness is linked to the African-Caribbean community's *deep suspicion of their own ethnic representatives*' (Werbner and Anwar, 1991, 17). Underlying such suspicion is the thought that the activists' involvement can and sometimes does lead to a 'sell-out' of the group and community aims when they use the community or a group's radical stance on particular issues to their own advantage, whether political, economic or both.

Outsider activists who may always remain on the periphery of the community *are most often suspected of collaboration*, [and] *accused of self-interested social climbing'* although in the long term it is more often these actors with a well travelled and outward looking political outlook and agenda who can transform local actions that may be quite parochial into more 'political' agendas.

> They may also play, however, a very significant mediatory role once anti-racist social movements gather momentum. It is often, indeed, leaders who are – at least in some significant cultural sense – of the 'periphery' who become the most radical activists and organisers of such social movements. It is they who most clearly 'politicise' culture, transforming it into an ideological agenda. (Werbner and Anwar, 1991, 22)

This book is arranged in four chapters. Chapter 1 provides an overview of Leeds African-Caribbean community groups using case studies and detailed analysis of eleven activists and their organisational activities. Chapter 2, 'Creating self-identity' provides an analysis of the interconnections between the reaffirmation of individual and group identity. Chapter 3, 'Black men's forums and African-Caribbean gender debates', explores the demands of African-Caribbean women for greater physical, economic and moral support from men of African descent. The response in the form of Black men's forum organisations is also analysed. Finally, Chapter 4 provides some concluding remarks and identifies the barriers which have to be overcome before sustained group action can be achieved.

Chapter 1

African-Caribbean groups: an overview

Chapters One and Two use fieldwork data from two case studies involving education and community radio stations and the detailed analysis of eleven purposely selected activists and their organisations from seven group categories illustrated in table 1. The organisations are the Afrikan Curriculum Development Association, Ashobi Animateurs, Barbados Women's Group, Black Mental Health Resource Centre, Chapeltown Business Centre, Chapeltown Independent After School, Kuffdem Arts, Leeds Black Elders Association, Freedom and Supreme FM, Mary Seacole Halfway House and The West Indian Family Counselling Service.

Table 1: Types of African-Caribbean community self-organised groups in Leeds	
Type of group	Number
Advice and advocacy	5
Arts	23
Education	9
Business and training	11
Health advice and support	4
Housing	6
Religion	7
Savings and finance	2
Social	13
Sport	5
Women's support groups	5
Others	3
Total	93

Education

The development of education groups in Leeds has a long history mirroring the national focus on African-Caribbean education achievements or, for the most part, under-achievement. Groups such as the United Caribbean Association (UCA), the West Indian Afro Brotherhood and UHURU Arts Group all played significant roles in combating the blatant racism in the state schools of Chapeltown and Harehills during the 1960s and 1970s. These organisations were involved in one of the key education group actions of the 1970s, where the Chapeltown Parents Action Group at Earl Cowper Middle School (now Hillcrest Primary School) organised a successful strike against a racist head teacher and for the improvement of teaching facilities.

> Members of the United Caribbean Association (UCA) and the West Indian Afro Brotherhood responded to the persistent complaints of parents about teachers' attitudes and the standard of education at Earl Cowper Middle School in the heart of Chapeltown. In particular, parents were able to quote overtly racist remarks by the headteacher. The remark attributed to the headteacher that appeared to be the most powerful mobliser of opinion was that 'black pupils have lower foreheads and less cranial capacity than the white pupils'. ... To focus the criticism of the parents, members of UCA and the Brotherhood helped set up the Chapeltown Parents' Action Group (CPAG). ... At a public meeting chaired by Mrs Odessa Stoute on Sunday 24 June 1973, the Action Group presented a list of educational demands which echoed in discussions nearly twenty years later:
>
> * to de-classify the school from a Middle to a Primary School
>
> * the removal of the head teacher
>
> * more Black governors 'who are interested in their own people'
>
> * better contact between the headmaster, parents and staff
>
> * improved internal facilities in the school
>
> * attempts must be made to slow down the fast teacher turnover in the school
>
> * more Black teachers
>
> * members of the Black community to be invited to speak to the children to give them more motivation
>
> * facilities and staff for extra teaching for the children in the evening. (Farrar, 1992, 56-57)

The strike was organised for Monday 25 June 1973 and parents kept their children away from school. Two months later the headmaster was transferred from the school – but he was promoted (Farrar, 1993, 23; see also *Chapeltown News*, July, August, October and November, 1993).

Education changes have mainly occurred due to the sustained efforts of the African and African-Caribbean people of Leeds. The outcome of these struggles has been the formation of nine African-Caribbean community based education self-organised groups who operate in Leeds Chapeltown and Harehills areas. Two groups provide supplementary education to children under 16 years: Chapeltown and Harehills Assisted Learning Computer School (CHALCS), and Chapeltown Independent After School (CIAS). Pre-Access and adult education are provided by the Afrikan Curriculum Development Association (ACDA), Chapeltown Black Writers' Group, Kisomo Umoja and Marcus Garvey Media (MGM). Help, advice and recruitment of Black governors is provided by the Black Governors Information Network. Chapeltown Young People's 10-2 Club is a youth club that is highly respected by 'street-wise' African-Caribbean youths, who meet on Wednesdays and Fridays between 10pm and 2am. The final group with an education function is Assegai, a networking organisation which aims to link the work of Leeds African-Caribbean education groups so as to improve organisational efficiency.

Several of these groups have an Africancentric focus and aim to establish permanent Africancentric schools. In the west Yorkshire region only one group, the Afrikan Building Collective (ABC group), can claim to have done this. The school is called PER ANKH or the house of life. It was originally based in Bradford at the Black Agenda library but relocated to Leeds in 1997. The opening of this school was signalled in the first edition of a Leeds community, education and cultural journal called Maroon.

> We are a group of Afrikan parents and potential parents who recognise that education of self and knowledge of self are the two central keys to Afrikan reconstruction in the 21st century. We have taken it upon ourselves to both educate our children and to build or purchase an environment suitable for an Afrikan school in which to exist.

Since being formed in September 1994 we have worked towards the point of conception which we are pleased to say happened on Monday 10 July 1995. On this day, thanks to the hard work put in by many Brothers and Sisters we are able to open the first independent Afrikan school in West Yorkshire. Provisionally called PER ANKH (The House of Life), the school opened in the library reading room of the Black Agenda Afrikan centred community library housed at 24 Barry Street, Bradford. (Maroon, May/June 1996. Alarm, November 1995 also described the opening of the school)

The African-Caribbean efforts in the area of education are a microcosm of the dilemma confronting African-Caribbeans in the area of public service provision, and connect with the balancing act individuals have to undertake in all areas of their everyday life. The dilemma is whether to opt for involvement in the present rules, regulations and administration systems or for rejecting the status quo and replacing it with alternatives (Goulbourne, 1993). In the field of education the dilemma is about whether concentrated, limited, individual and group energies should be channelled into efforts to try and change the existing education structures, or whether it would be more worthwhile in the long term to begin the process of creating alternatives (such as Black schools) to existing statutory provision. African-Caribbean groups have tended to use both strategies. They intervene in an effort to make the existing state system more user friendly towards African-Caribbean children and adult learners and they are also trying to create autonomous schools, support services and networks providing an alternative to existing state education. Although different groups will place greater emphasis on each strategy, some organisations such as the Afrikan Building Collective opt for alternative provisions as the core of their activities.

African and African-Caribbean immigrant groups in the UK have a powerful allegiance and a firm belief in the power of education for individual and group self-advancement. First generation settlers have sacrificed their time and efforts in the belief that once their children have been integrated in the adopted society, particularly if they can gain academic success, it would be more difficult, if not impossible, to deny them equal treatment regarding employment, housing or general self-acceptance in UK society. Generally the 'first generation' were prepared to 'take the shit' in the hope their children would rise.

Supplementary schools are usually not a rejection of the value of education or the idea of a meritocratic society. The supplementary or extra schooling ethos is geared to helping African-Caribbean children gain equal access to the education services provided by the state. This belief system is not at odds with the concept of education. The debates and struggles are focused on the degree of access and the curricula that are taught. Education is a public provision forming a part of an important pathway to gain valuable life skills. To succeed in this system requires knowledge of the rules of the organisation and the ability to make effective challenges. The main African-Caribbean focus is to change the existing education system so that they can gain equal access, equal support once they are in the system, and also to achieve a curriculum that takes account of African experiences and histories. African-Caribbean parents wish their children to succeed. It is because the existing services have failed African-Caribbean youth that parents and pupils and other concerned individuals have been prompted to form educational pressure groups to challenge the existing educational provision. Groups such as the Afrikan Curriculum Development Association, Assegai and Marcus Garvey Media operate with long term aims. Not only are they advocates and supplementary course providers but they hope in time to create the environment where there will be no need for African-Caribbean children to attend the existing state maintained schools. This is perhaps a convenient place to pause for an analysis of the concept of Afrocentricity or Africancentric focus referred to earlier.

Afrocentricity
Africans of the world-wide diaspora (including African-Caribbeans) have an ongoing project concerned with the re-establishment of an Afrocentric (or Africancentric) culture but still have to come to terms with existing realities and are therefore forced to adopt sometimes *'seemingly contradictory strategies of seeking to withdraw from areas of mainstream society while struggling to participate more meaningfully in other areas'* (Goulbourne, 1993, 183). Positive African-Caribbean survival in the west entails a reaffirmation of historic African cultural heritage whilst down-grading or sometimes rejecting the western Eurocentric or European aspects of their history and present condi-

tion. This concept can be interpreted as an attempt at rediscovery as means of survival through 'correct' activity (Ani, 1994; Asante, 1992 and 1988; Browder, 1989).

Although not formally acknowledging western theories, Afrocentricity contains the threads of ideas from critical theory and post-modernist thoughts. From critical theory came the emphasis on praxis (activity) through a critical understanding of the individual and group life-world. Change occurs not only through this understanding and activity in the public sphere but is also conditional on a changed private and public lifestyle. This type of inner change is similar to the thoughts of Franz Fanon (1986 and 1965) in the 1950s and 1960s, and the Black consciousness movement in southern Africa initiated by Steven Biko in the 1970s, where worthwhile and lasting activity and change had to be preceded by a changed consciousness (Woods, 1978). This changed inner consciousness preceded activity. It is the casting off of an inner yoke of psychological oppression to arrive at the belief that the African is once more the subject of history with agency, rather than an object doomed to passivity. For Afrocentricity, this new concept of self-worth is based on a true historical analysis of past African events that have helped to shape the world, even though in the recording of European history the legacy of African ideas and actions have been unrecognised or distorted (James, 1992; Diop, 1974).

From post-modernism came the issues of particularism or plurality, and the critique of the damaging effects of modern information networks, particularly visual images which provided individuals and groups with distorted visions of themselves and their past history. This creates and sustains the idea of their impotence in the future. With the exception of Melucci (1989) and Jamerson (1984), Afrocentricity differs from the post-modernist approach in the Afrocentric insistence and faith in positive by-ways out of the information debacle. The Afrocentric way out is a critique of information presented from the standpoint of the Eurocentric world where past and present progressive ideas and actions are presented as stemming from the European world. This is negation of the rich heritage of Africa and Africans past, present and future. Cheika Anta Diop expressed it thus:

> For us the return to Egypt in all domains is the necessary condition for reconciling African civilization with history, in order to be able to con-

struct a body of modern human sciences, in order to renovate African culture. Far from being a revelling in the past, a look towards the Egypt of antiquity is the best way to conceive and build our cultural pride. In reconceived and renewed African culture, Egypt will play the same role that Greco-Latin antiquity plays in Western culture. (Diop, 1991, 3)

Afrocentricity thus places great emphasis on rediscovering and recording this historical past, particularly information pertaining to Kemet – the ancient name of Egypt (Asante, 1992; Browder, 1989). This is used as means of refocusing the linear line of world (particularly western) historical knowledge to enable Africans to use this knowledge and re-centre themselves in the world as active and constructive agents. In the long term such a changed concept of knowledge formation – the wide acceptance of the true historical roots of western knowledge and species, an African-centred scheme rather than a European-centred approached, is akin to the transformation from an earth (geo-centric) to a sun (helio-centric) centred universe advocated by Ptolomy and Aristotle. The geo-centric explanation placed the earth at the centre of the universe with all other planets and stars revolving around it in a circular motion. The helio-centric world view placed the sun at the centre of the known universe, with the other planets including the earth revolving in elliptical orbits at different speeds around it (Koestler, 1968). The new knowledge is a threat to the old world order because acceptance will literally turn the world upside down.

Afrocentric writers and activists such as Marimba Ani – formerly known as Patricia Newton (1994) – Del Jones (1993), Molefi Asante (1992), Anthony Browder (1989), Rosalind Jefferies and Nana Sekhmet believe it is not enough to know and write about knowing. An individual has to act. Power comes from de-centring Eurocentric knowledge and replacing it with Afrocentric history – it is historical knowledge used in the present as a catalyst for activity. Other academic/activists such as Hakim Adi and Marika Sherwood of the Black and Asian Studies Association use more recent knowledge of Black presence in the UK as a tool for replacing Africans in European history into situations from which they have been mostly erased. This knowledge is also intended as a framework for present activities. Unlike many theories of action, Afrocentric ideas and actions are not confined to the universities or an educated elite but are widely known in the African and African-Caribbean communities in the UK and USA. It has a further edge, due to its organic intellectuals who are of African descent (Gramsci, 1987). They are of the people, they share the same history, they initiate and are involved in practical activities, they live the theory and their perceptions of life are based on African concepts and historical knowledge. But Afrocentric ideas have been criticised by theorists such as Paul Gilroy (1993) and bell hooks (1991) who believe the Afrocentric quest for authenticity and uniformity is a myth.

Community radio

The second case study concerns two community radio stations. Supreme and Freedom FM are two of a total of four self financing African-Caribbean/African radio stations operating in the Chapeltown and Harehills areas of Leeds. The aim of Freedom FM is to use musical forms to help to create an audience possessing a positive sense of African and African-Caribbean identities. I suspect similar aims would be endorsed by the activists at Supreme FM, although their musical programmes were focused on 'slack' music, with lyrics featuring sex and violence and disparaging women, so doing little to affirm positive African identities. Supreme FM has been going for about nine years, and was one of the earliest community radio stations in Leeds. It is primarily a music station, ranging from American soul to reggae, and does not have a broadcasting licence. According to a former disc jockey (DJ):

> Supreme FM was set-up by ... local people to basically play African-Caribbean music and do a little discussion to give exposure to local DJs, and to do some basic advertising. (5 February 1995)

In the 1960s and 1970s Supreme FM would have been termed a 'pirate' radio station, but in Chapeltown and Harehills, Supreme and the handful of similar radio stations are generally called 'community radio stations'. Although the station's transmitter can reach areas such as Burley, six miles away, in 1995 Supreme's listening audience was mainly African-Caribbean young men living in Chapeltown and Harehills. The station's twenty voluntary DJs (three women and seventeen men) were either 'unemployed' or survived on the edge of mainstream employment. They were mainly of African-Caribbean descent although there were one Asian and one European DJ who played jazz records. Most were in their early twenties and were born in and around Leeds.

About six years ago the station personnel began to think critically about the type of music they presented. The DJs tried to cut down on 'pum-pum' or 'slack' records that make explicit sexual references and endorse interpersonal violence. Music with 'slack rhythms' and messages have been replaced by more 'uplifting' or 'crucial' records that can help create a positive sense of self for the whole African-Caribbean community. Now African-Caribbean women and men can find in their radio station an affirmation of their community and a sense of self-worth and respect. It is interesting to note that before the discussions about the content of the music, the three women DJs at Supreme FM also played 'slack music' without questioning it.

Before the musical content of Supreme FM changed there was one programme that stood out from the rest. This was a 'progressive' and 'radical' music and discussion programme, hosted by an education activist known locally to his listeners as the 'African teacher'. This African/African-Caribbean programme was unique, broadcasting discussion and critical analysis of local, national and international issues and events affecting the lives of Africans and African-Caribbeans linked with African, African-American and African-Caribbean musical forms. The 'African teacher' classified his music mix as African music from the continent and the diaspora. He was adamant that there was no disunity between these various music forms because all were African. He promoted similar ideas about the people of African descent world-wide – they should also all be classified as Africans.

The African teacher's Sunday programme on Supreme occupied a three hour slot from 12-3pm including thirty minutes of discussion. Topics such as analyses of the civil war in Rwanda and educational issues with children from the local supplementary Saturday school were debated. Other issues included nutrition and fashion tips, and invited local and national guests would regularly appear on the programme. This music and discussion format ran for three years, although the presenter operated on a voluntary basis and remained unpaid for his education radio work. He said that his involvement in this form of medium was due to his strong desire to expose African-Caribbeans to African cultures, African teachings and African analysis, which he achieved by a skilful mixture of various Black arts expressive performance arts including jazz, poetry by Sister 'P', Linton Kwesi Johnson and Jean Binter Breeze, combined with soca music and social commentary. He believed it important to break up the constant flow of African music while aiming to engender a positive sense of an African self through combining music with radical discussions relevant to the African and African-Caribbean local audience. He was – and is – very much aware of the apathy and divisions that exist in both communities. This can manifest itself in three forms, (a) the splits between African and African-Caribbean people who have internalised negative stereotypes of each other, (b) the sometimes narrow range of music forms enjoyed by some sections of each grouping, and (c) the short attention spans that discussion can generate compared to the pull of Black music forms. So he had to mix the various arts formats, lest some or all of his programme content be rejected by sections of his audience. For instance, if only African music was played or discussions went on for over half an hour, both the music and the discussions might be rejected by his audience. He was adamant that: '... *if you are trying to get them to accept African music you have to present them with all those interesting things to do'* (5 February 1995).

Some African-Caribbean listeners asked the programme DJ to play more popular or commercial African music with which they were more familiar, such as that of the South African Miriam Makeba, rather than non-commercial African material. It is significant that such comments were not made live on air during the programme's phone-in slot but in private conversations with the presenter. There was not much telephone feed-back to the studio while the programme was being broadcast, but the little there was mostly agreed with the programme content and offered only minimal contradictions. Women made the most calls to the programme but most feed-back came from personal contact on the streets with listeners (usually older African-Caribbeans) who said they enjoyed the programme. The 'African teacher' told me that:

Africans I meet will say to me 'the programme was good but you play too much reggae', ... and that I seem to hold the fort for African-Caribbean people, and that my focus is for African-Caribbeans. But there are Africans [musicians] who do not get any play at all so that I should focus on African music and cut out all the other music (5 February 1995).

While this radical music discussion programme was unique in the format of Supreme FM's output another local community radio station had become a leading exponent of such 'conscious' or 'serious' music and discussion output. According to the African teacher there was only two other programmes on community radio that were similar to his. They were both on Freedom FM. One was hosted by the 'African Herbsman', and the other by the 'African Principal', and both DJs played 'rasta conscious music'. With the exception of these three programmes, there was a dearth of political discussion on all the community radio stations. In many instances politics only surfaced in the form of advertising for specific local events such as education meetings or conferences.

In addition to their time spent presenting music programmes on Supreme FM, the DJs would be linked to or 'front' local 'sound systems'. A sound system can be compared to a powerful disco record playing system except that the African-Caribbean systems are famous for their large speaker boxes, which have the capacity to deliver massive power and deep base lines. The concept originated from Jamaica and, as in the Caribbean, the systems and their DJs or 'toasters' can acquire cult followings of near religious significance. This was an important aspect of their activities because it was here that they were not only heard but seen. Such exposure offered opportunities to be paid for their appearancy – unlike their radio work. The radio and public sound system events nurtured each other and enhanced the reputation of the performers.

Competition between local DJs and those from other cities were encouraged by the music activists and their audiences. There are endless debates about who is the hardest DJ – who has access to the latest and raunchiest discs that should be played on the loudest and heaviest base lines? But this provokes another question: 'who has the best stereo system to be able to reproduce the required music format'? To try and settle this, DJs from, say, Manchester and Birmingham would be invited to a DJ competition party at the West Indian Centre in Leeds. Each DJ would arrive with their own stereo system and be given the opportunity to play their records. At the end of the evening the audience decided the winner. During the month of August local DJs such as 'Sweet G' and 'DOC', and others from community radio stations in Leeds including Supreme also played in Potternewton Park at the annual Leeds Carnival events, earning in the order of £100-£200. Similar to their contemporaries from other UK cities and towns, the Leeds DJs travelled around the country and played at different venues – 'that's how they survive'.

In early 1994 the African Teacher moved from Supreme FM to Freedom FM where for two years he hosted a music and discussion programme similar to the format he had created at Supreme. This move was partly by invitation from key activists at Freedom FM but was precipitated also because of Supreme's difficulty in maintaining regular programming. He told me that sometimes he would arrive at the Supreme FM transmitter but could not get in because there was no one there to let him in. On other occasions broadcasting equipment was stolen or the station was raided by the broadcasting authorities, who would then confiscate equipment. Either way, the station could not broadcast and was off the airwaves. In contrast Freedom FM appeared to be on-air whenever he turned on his radio. He was of the opinion that:

> Freedom FM was the most positive radio station or community station we have because it takes its line from Rastafarian consciousness. (5 February 1995)

Freedom FM appeared to be more organised than the other African-Caribbean local radio stations. Freedom FM was, moreover, motivated by a Rastafarian philosophy and it was working towards becoming legitimate by acquiring a broadcasting licence. According to the African Teacher, the other radio stations were not interested in such legitimation, perhaps because they lacked commitment, skill and knowledge. He described the goal of Freedom FM as being to act as a movement to *create a situation where the message of love, the message of solidarity, the message of possessiveness towards Africa and African people through Rastafarianism and conscious music will be given a permanent place*.

Generally the DJs have an affinity with the local African-Caribbean community for several reasons. They form a bond with their audience because most of them were born in the local community, went to school with the audience and play records that appeal to a mainly young disenfranchised African-Caribbean male clientele. The DJs may be considered heroes because they operate on the edge of legality outside the present broadcasting laws that may be considered as oppressive or at least 'white men's laws'. The activists were not involved in mainstream employment and their audience would understand their efforts to avoid becoming involved in work they considered menial or demeaning. The endeavour was to find methods of cultural and financial survival considered meaningful in their own terms rather than being forced to accept dead-end jobs that were seen as a return to slavery. Activist and audience affinity were therefore based on a shared history and the current cultural, political and financial redefinition. There was a shared lifestyle, with music acting as the key signifier. Music helped to create and sustain a bond among African-Caribbeans, it relieved tensions created in the private and public spheres of daily activities. While many areas of possible public activity successes in education and employment spheres might appear closed or restricted for African-Caribbeans, music and its attendant lifestyle forms may open up possibilities for creativity and renewed self-image, and could be used as a focus for a type of resistance culture that it is difficult for outsiders to understand or penetrate. The community radio presenter could be the outward or public expression of this alternative means of survival in the inner cities, but there are many other methods of group activity and survival strategies – as we shall see.

Profile of activists

Table 2 indicates the gender, age range and place of birth of the eleven Leeds African-Caribbean group activists I interviewed, using a semi-structured format. Four were women and seven were men. Most (6) were between 40 and 59 years old, three were between 20 and 39 and two were over 60. The most common place of birth was Barbados (4), followed by Jamaica (2) and the UK (2), with St. Kitts-Nevis, Montserrat and Ghana each claiming one. All are motivated by inter-linked 'political' agendas. These include spirituality, the need to initiate change and have a voice that is heard, the creation of strong individual, family and ethnic group identities, and the quest to connect people to positive aspects of their culture. Some sought to use education and Black arts for individual and collective changes, promoting knowledge which could provide the will and practical information to enable a return to Africa. The response of a 40 year old housing activist is typical of the unselfish drive the activists display. He came to the UK when he was eleven years old, does not have a personal goal and believes he is a simple person whose only requirements are to live a happy life and 'get on' with people.

Table 2: Gender, age range and place of birth of eleven Leeds African-Caribbean group activists

Gender		Age range			Place of birth
Women	*Men*	*20-39*	*40-59*	*60+*	
1	-	-	1	-	Jamaica
-	1	1	-	-	UK
1	-	-	-	1	Barbados
1	-	1	-	-	UK
-	1	-	1	-	St Kitts-Nevis
-	1	-	1	-	Barbados
-	1	-	1	-	Ghana
-	1	1	-	-	Jamaica
-	1	-	-	1	Barbados
-	1	-	1	-	Barbados
1	-	-	1	-	Montserrat
4	**7**	**3**	**6**	**2**	**Total**

His major concern is to assist the creation of Black unity by the formation of proactive groups. Blacks should not be ashamed of their roots and values and should learn to appreciate their culture. Groups should create the forum to assist this process. He believes that Africans and African-Caribbeans are currently lost and scattered and so have become easy targets for potential destruction.

> But for Black people my aim is to see us unite as Black people, taking on board the issues that face us more seriously, and to form groups. Not reactionary groups but proactive groups, our own groups. Because as African-Caribbeans I don't think we have our own groups.

We adopted the European type of groups and assimilated into the European type of culture, and we have forgotten our culture, ... we are ashamed of our culture, our roots. To me it would be about forming groups that get people back to our values and appreciate that our values are strong, and that we have got something to offer, and we intend talking about Africa and looking back to Africa for our future – our leadership. ... I would like to be instrumental within a group that actually try and bring that about. ... Because for me, we are lost, we are scattered, and scattered people are easy to pick off, and I think that's what happening to us as Black people. (Housing activist, 15 May 1995)

Two activists, one born in Barbados and the other in Jamaica, came to live in Leeds when they were children. In this study's terms, they are insider activists, because they have spent most of their life in Leeds. Unlike some insiders they are receptive to new ideas and actions from African and African-Caribbean newcomers. All the other activists interviewed had a history of involvement in voluntary or statutory organisations before coming to Leeds, or began their activities when they settled there. Such was the case of a Barbados-born bus driver who spent 37 years as a rank-and-file trade union activist in Leeds.

For the most of my time working for the transport industry I was a trade union activist and started as a shop steward, and particularly started to take an interest in minority affairs because at that time what I noticed in the early stages [was] that there was in some cases discrimination, and in some cases patronisation. ... I was brought in by one of the full-time trade union official to assist in some way, to help redress the balance, and I was at that from 1958 until ... about 37 years I was a trade unionist. (Social group activist, 23 March 1995)

Other activists had been involved in organisations in the Caribbean and in Ghana and Sierra Leone. In St Kitts-Nevis, where he was born, one respondent was a junior leader in a youth organisation called Fisowa. This group originated in the USA and had satellite organisations in Scotland concentrating on sporting development, education and social and cultural issues. Another activist maintained that he *'was a product of the neo-colonial education system'* in Ghana and so his political involvement and understanding of African events had been limited accordingly. He conceded that his world during the 1960s and 1970s was very Christianised. He was in the school choir but managed to gain progressive thoughts by reading the *Readers Digest* and discussing its ideas with his friends. Although the Digest issues were not usually linked to contemporary events in Ghana, he and his friends were nevertheless able to *'identify with Blackness and* [tried] *to be Africacentric, a bit'*. Interestingly, he had been educated at what was considered one of the 'best' preparatory boarding schools in Ghana, and where speaking African languages was suppressed.

> I was in a place with ministers' sons and daughters. English was compulsory, and if you spoke African languages and you were caught they would hang a board around your neck saying 'I will not speak vernacular anymore', and you paid one pence, which was a lot of money for me at that time. ... You had that tag on for a week, sometimes two weeks, wearing it all the time. You wore it every time you were out. (Education and music activist, 5 February 1995)

This activist is very Africancentric now, and well able to transfer this approach to the education, cultural and artistic organisations in which he is involved. Another activist, born in the UK of Sierra Leonean and Scottish ancestry, had spent sixteen years in Sierra Leone before coming to Leeds in 1987. In Sierra Leone, Guinea, the Gambia and Liberia he had gathered the foundations of his world view and begun his involvement and interest in publishing, writing and politics.

> ... I was always writing. I won a first prize intermediate for a Commonwealth poetry competition [1971 or 1972] and that gave me confidence to write some poetry, lead on really to journalism. I was constantly writing for newspapers in Sierra Leone, opposition ones and the government ones (Arts and education activist, 20 February 1995).

Other activists were involved in church organisations, an African-Caribbean women's group, student societies such as an African-Caribbean society and student liaison committees. A Leeds education activist stated that his first voluntary group involvement occurred in the early 1970s when he came to the UK to live in Liverpool. He was involved in an organisation called the West Indian Cricket Club. This organisation, similar to those in Leeds, (Caribbean Cricket Club) London and other major UK cities at the time, helped to organise dances, social outings, assistance with funeral expenses, and generally assisted new arrivals from the Caribbean with housing, jobs and social needs. Especially during the 1950s and 1960s this type of cultural and welfare organisation was the major source for *'networking within the* [African-Caribbean] *community'*. For instance, *'that was the only*

source where Black people used to meet in Liverpool in the early days'
(Education activist, 6 April 1995).

Activists' analyses of African-Caribbean group actions

Like most committed activists, the goals of the community activists
are both immediate and long term. They have to deal with situations
in the 'here-and-now' to help themselves and others to survive and
remain sane in what they consider to be a sometimes insane environment of racism and indifference. They are generally unconcerned with
the theoretical constitution of the work they are involved with in their
various groups. In addition to their general unease about the niceties
of theory, most of them are unaware of many of the academic
explanations such as critical theory or social movements that have
been credited with providing insights concerning group actions. This
lack of acknowledgement of theory does not imply that such knowledge has not percolated into their lives – only that they are unaware
of how knowledge is transmitted. Activists do indeed use academic
concepts or offer explanations in support of their rejection of particular concepts such as class theory, although they may not realise
where and how they acquired the information. However, just because
their insights may be incoherent or contradictory, this should not dis-
qualify their ideas and analyses. Their ideas help them to determine
the actions in which they are involved. Therefore, in keeping with
these aims the data below will detail the reasons the activists give for
group actions.

Group actions create a sense of security and strength, unity and a
feeling of belonging where people with common interests are able to
act together. People in groups believe they have the ability to change
existing structures because together they can make things happen.
Group action occurs because individuals are able to relate to others
through common ideals of need and shared ideas. Different groups
are formed because humans are diverse and people with commonalty
tend to stick together. Individuals tend to look for support from others
in their own ethnic or peer groups. Sometimes people belong to a
group for reasons of personal self-interest such as assisting their own
social mobility. One activist described examples of this that he had
observed in groups based in Chapeltown and Harehills. For instance,

members of the building co-operative Frontline Self-Build Housing Association are together because they wanted to gain employment and earn an income. The 10-2 Club members organise in an effort to gain resources such as games for their youth club. At the Mary Seacole Nurses Association, people skilled in nursing are trying to develop a service for older members of the African-Caribbean community to enrich their lives so as *'to create a better social position for these people'*. It was agreed that although African-Caribbean group actions occurred for a number of reasons including self-interest, there were certainly strong motives of assisting the wider group or community. Characteristic of this wider altruistic approach are individuals who come together to form sub-groups based on variables such as age and gender. Where formations are related to age, specifically the older people, it could be for the benefit of reliving shared cultures and experiences from their country of origin. Such groupings are able to share personal recollections about present situations in the Caribbean when group members return from visits and recall their experiences. Individuals align themselves with others with whom they can feel comfortable or have a measure of shared interests or concerns. According to one education activist (6 April 1995):

> You look for a group that you feel happy with when you also trying to relax, socialise. Because although you might got a group that you do a lot of work for, fund-raising activities, decorating, painting, you still always look for a group that at the end of the day when it's time for you to wind-down and have a nice socialise, have a drink, have something to eat, have a chat, have a dance, talk about old times, ... everybody looks for that type of group, ... that they can recharge the batteries, and that's what I look for in a group.

The speaker is also a member of one of the six African-Caribbean organisations in Leeds set up in relation to their place of birth in the Caribbean: the Barbados Association, the Barbados Choir, the Barbados Women's Group, the Jamaica Society, the Jamaica Choir, and the St. Kitts-Nevis Association, which can be termed island groups, are no longer reproduced as an organisational tool. The emphases now appear to focus on united forms of actions encompassed under group names such as African-Caribbean, Afro-Caribbean and unity. Nevertheless these island groups have survived although it can be argued that they cater for an ageing and disappearing clientele. But this education activist argued against the notion that island groups will fade out because he believes that some young people regard their parents' country of origin as their own home, and are keen to sustain the island groups by their participation.

> The younger people although they were not born in the West Indies, most of them know of the West Indies and although the organisations will take a different direction the organisation wont die, ... but they wont have the same sentimentality to the roots. (6 April 1995)

Some of those who were born in the UK have visited the Caribbean and have expressed their possible intentions to settle there in the future. The activist believes these younger activists will not change the norms of the island associations because they view places such as Jamaica and Barbados as their homes. These optimistic feelings are tempered by the realisation that it is difficult, if not impossible, to motivate young African-Caribbean men to sustain their participation in African-Caribbean organisations – whereas African-Caribbean women have a high rate of involvement in group activities. An activist in the Barbados Women's Group mentioned a group of young Barbadians in London who are keen to continue organising based on a location identity, although she did not believe such feelings are as strong for African-Caribbeans in Leeds.

> ... there is a group in London called the Younger Youth Group, and that's going quite well. (31 July 1995)

There was some agreement with the premise that African-Caribbean groups are both active and reactive where their actions are mainly in response to the racism faced in their daily lives. Although strong feelings were expressed about the lack of proactive inventiveness:

> ... they're not creating anything; it's all reactive (Art and youth activist, 20 February 1995)...

not all activity was reactive:

> ... some of it's proactive because something like ACDA [the Afrikan Curriculum Development Association] and – it's a chicken before the egg whichever way it comes, because you could look at a situation and say this is proactive, to respond, to actually deal with that situation. Reactive response could be that recently there was some incident in Chapeltown with some young people being carted off by the van-load, ... the police was supposed to have stopped a young person and others leapt out of nowhere and suddenly started attacking them,

so there is some agitation then within the community to deal with the situation. There is the youth work that takes place, which is a preventative measure, and I am thinking like the youth club as part of that, to try and prevent young people getting involved in negative situations with the police, so that's proactive. ... Palace Youth Project is proactive and some of it was there to respond to issues as they arose – so I think there is both [proactive and reactive group responses] if there wasn't racism, if there wasn't oppression and African and African-Caribbean children got the education they need, and they weren't picked on by the police, and we got better housing and better employment, then there would be more proactivity as opposed to reactivity (Education activist, 9 February 1995).

Group activity is considered as creating a place of safety and a form of innate herding instinct where individual abilities can be pooled and the best attributes of the individual have an arena to grow and develop.

We do not always reach our potential. Then as we get into a group with the group dynamics and are called upon to do things, that brings out the best in us (Island group activist, 31 July 1995).

A health professional activist used her own experiences as a starting point to explain the need for collective support and actions. She is sure that her reasons for being involved with African-Caribbean groups is due to her initial isolation from the wider Black community, because her parents 'kept themselves to themselves'. She was jolted by the blatant racism she experienced when she went to study in York. She felt 'unsafe and threatened, and tried to seek out people who I could relate to'. She felt a great need to be involved in Black groups 'to be with my own people'. She soon 'had a sense of feeling whole, feeling comfortable' because the isolation of coping in predominately white areas and the need to sometimes put on a mask when she was involved in white groups, were lifted. While she recognised the wider political motives for group involvement, her personal experiences of 'alienation' forced her to concede that the initial urge for group involvement comes from a personal need or statement (3 August 1995).

Class theory is rejected as explaining the motivation and sustenance for African-Caribbean group actions.

I am not quite sure whether African-Caribbean people get together on the basis of class, I think it's on the basis of oppression and then the groups will be fragmented and splinter off to deal with various issues. You could get a whole group of people together and then there are various issues that come up. Some will be keen on education, some on gender, sexuality, I think the class thing is reductionist. (Education activist, 9 February 1995)

An education and arts activist believed that group resistance is based on resistance to attacks on young African-Caribbean people. Class based analysis is considered as insufficient explanation, because *'class does not motive them'*. However, another activist who is involved in arts and education groups accepted that exclusion theory can provide possible tools by which to analyse African-Caribbean actions.

Insiders and outsiders

The creation of group cohesion is fraught with difficulties which have to be overcome. Racism is a form of rejection that makes it difficult to know who can be trusted. If an actor is constantly brutalised and rejected, it is difficult to remain loving and open to others, and difficult to practise self-love. The situation is similar in South Africa, where the past history built on apartheid had a strong violent element. Violence became one of the most important means of retaining Europeanised political and economic control, and it also became a part of Black African resistance. The official ending of apartheid has not completely ended the resorting to violence as a method of political economy, because a brutalised environment is likely to create brutalised people.

The mistrust of outsiders in the Leeds African-Caribbean community owes something to the specific history of African-Caribbean residence in the city after the Second World War. It is a history of isolation and a fight for spatial identity against patronisation and informers. The fight against these events caused some community individuals to adopt insular values. It has been argued that when individuals believe they cannot control the wider events in the world around them they tend to reduce their world to an area they can more easily understand and control (Castells, 1983). Their world becomes the local community. This might consist of the people in the locality who share the same ethnicity and a network of social ties, have been involved in local community organisations or may have been school mates. This world can be reduced further to include only members of immediate family and ultimately of the self alone. With such reductionism it becomes problematic to venture beyond self to face risks about who can or cannot be trusted. A woman education activist who came to Leeds after living most of her life in other northern cities provides an account of her first impressions of the insular environment she encountered from some individuals in the Leeds African-Caribbean community.

> When I first moved to Leeds I was working at the Palace Youth Project in Chapeltown, and from my discussions with young people, ... and people say, ... younger than 18, maybe 18-35 or plus age group. I found them to be quite insular in that they were very sort of protective towards Chapeltown, and as an outsider you could not say – on occasions I was told that I was an outsider and therefore I didn't know about the area and what was happening or what was going on. ... People talked, but if I made any comments on incidents or tried to comment on what was happening in Chapeltown in comparison to somewhere else I was sometimes told that I wasn't from around here so I didn't know what was happening or what had happened before, and I'm not a Leeds person, I'm not from Chapeltown, and basically shut-up because you don't know anything. (9 February 1995)

She had not encountered quite such an insular reaction in local African-Caribbean groups outside Leeds, although she realises that this was because, except when at university, she had not moved into an enclosed community before she came to Leeds. She told me that she had:

> ... never moved into something that's tight. ... It may seem loose in some ways but it's very tight. I did feel like an outsider coming in. (9 February 1995)

Although at the time of interview (February 1995) she had lived in Leeds for five years and had been actively involved in a number of African-Caribbean groups and other campaigning organisations, she still encountered rejection of her ideas and actions 'from particular individuals'. She tended to accept that tensions were inevitable between the newcomers or 'outsiders' and the African-Caribbean residents born in Leeds or living there for a considerable time, the 'insiders'. She understands that the newcomer has to be aware of local conditions in order to judge what was and what was not acceptable.

To realise any hopes of being an effective interventionist, outsiders should be versed in the history of the local area and the earlier concerns and activities of the local community before they can successfully introduce new strategies for community development.

> Because as I see it you can protect your space, but for me as an outsider, I have no allegiance to it, but I can come in and make suggestions about how things could possibly be improved, or how to deal with a certain situation, and then I get some of this history and how people have tried to deal with things in the past, and that they don't deal with things a certain way, and I can appreciate that because I'm not from around [here]. (Education activist, 9 February 1995)

We saw that this education activist experienced the notion of what can be termed an insider/outsider syndrome when she was a (Coventry) university student. She was rejected not by visiting African students but by African and African-Caribbean students at the university, *'the ones who were probably born here and who had been in the UK for some time'.*

> ... you certainly felt that you should not be there; 'what are you doing there'? ... I put it down to – they are at university – WOW – and what's this other Black person coming here for. ... It was something about being Black and being in a spot, a little place that you didn't want anyone else to come in and disrupt or mess up.

> [The activist agrees that action of this type can be caused by a fear of numbers] ... because it's something that's being perpetuated by white society anyway. You can have one or two Blacks working in an environment, and that's OK, but you certainly don't want lots of them in there because there is bound to be trouble. (9 February 1995)

Some of the existing African-Caribbean students might have believed that with the increase in the numbers of Black students at the university their presence would be negatively highlighted. An arts and education activist (20 February 1995) related how in Chapeltown some insiders might confront outsiders with statements such as:

> What's it to you what happens in the community – what do you know about it? ... I've played in the playground here, you don't know. ... [However, these parochial statements do not unnerve him because] that sought of thing don't worry me, if anything it gives me a fresher eye and they the more jaded eye. I think that's an advantage.

Socio-economic position and political consciousness

The issues concerning socio-economic positions and individual and collective actions are less polarised. Class consciousness and political consciousness do not have an innate relationship with an actor's class, educational achievement, financial or social status in UK society. There is no categorical imperative (Kant, 1973) implying that a person's political behaviour will automatically correspond to their social position, although this can be used as a basic explanatory tool. For example, peasants occupy a very stratified world, subject to, the variances of more powerful groups. Generally peasant groupings, poor, middle and rich tend to act in their own interests, sometimes conflicting with the interests of their neighbours. Peasant unity is usually assured when they believe their world is threatened and their whole way of life and possibly their lives are likely to be destroyed. In such a scenario sub-group differences are over-ridden by the need to act as an ethnic unit to ensure the survival of the group as a whole (Wolf, 1987).

Similarly, African-Caribbeans do not act in the classical Marxist sense of envisaging inter-group conflicts based on the sub-group's class position or relationship to the means of production and exchange. Because they have to deal with racism in western countries where they are minorities, African-Caribbeans tend to act in a similar manner to peasant actors – they consider that regardless of the socio-economic position of individuals in the ethnic group, all members must act for the common good or they will all be destroyed. Destruction can indeed be physical, when a way of life is ended by physically terminating the lives of the members of the group. But destruction can be more subtle, due not to physical force but rather the destruction of the psychological, the mind – thus undermining the moral fabric of individuals and ultimately the group itself. How can individuals who survive such attacks continue to cope with the knowledge that by opting out of the struggle they assisted the demise of their ethnic group and its way of life? In western societies racism is inescapable because it does not respect wealth or socio-economic characteristics of African or African-Caribbean individuals. What is important is the group status, and in this scheme people of African descent have low status. Group status is directly linked to individual status: material wealth or educational success does not completely mitigate or change attitudes to the individual's ethnic origins.

African-Caribbeans in Leeds act on issues affecting their ethnicity. Their impetus to organise is based on their collective identity and collective suffering as African people living in the western diaspora. The force of discrimination in the UK drove together African-Caribbeans of middle and working 'class' social groups in situations that did not occur in the Caribbean. Their collective experiences of racism broke down this separation and encouraged people of African/ Caribbean descent to come together in cultural, political and organisational terms. According to a Barbados born activist who came to the UK in 1956:

> You would find someone who could have been a teacher ... as against the ordinary labourer, where at home he wouldn't normally mix or cross path with each other. I think those people came here with similar ideas but the discrimination that they had to face was a leveller, they didn't have much choice. ... In this sense discrimination has brought us closer together. (23 March 1995)

He believes this scenario is as relevant today as it was as a catalyst in the erosion of socio-economic differences in the 1950s and 1960s. Whilst there are tensions, sometimes mistrust and differences of political emphasis between African-Caribbeans of different socio-economic positions, their over-riding aims are to raise the esteem of the members of their ethnic group and the status of the whole group. This is not to deny that socio-economic differences are problematic and difficult to overcome, as the information from two London male graduates illustrates. Education is sometimes viewed as the panacea for many of the issues plaguing people of African descent in inner-city areas of UK society. Whilst a change in socio-economic circumstances can have positive effects, such as a wider choice of job opportunities and possible place of residence, such changes can also create problems. These two African-Caribbean graduates both encountered difficulties finding a place for themselves in either working or middle class sections of the African-Caribbean community. They felt rejected by working class African-Caribbeans, whom they classified as resentful of their educational success, and they in turn found it difficult to relate to many of the interests of their working class colleagues. It could be expected that they would have been more comfortable in the company of those of similar socio-economic status, but this did not appear to be so. Many of the middle class African-Caribbeans they encountered were only interested in discussing and parading their material wealth and achievements and the respondents were adamant that they were not prepared to tolerate such behaviour and values among their graduate colleagues. While the two graduates appeared sincere in their commitment to try and establish meaningful relationships in the community of their ethnicity their change in socio-economic standing and their commitment to a non-individualist ethic set them apart and hindered their re-integration in the African-Caribbean community (8 August 1995).

Sometimes this education and cultural divide can be viewed as an inter-generational gap related to place of birth. One education activist placed on record the universally accepted African-Caribbean belief that there were two types of Caribbean knowledge in the African-Caribbean community in the UK: one voiced by those born in the Caribbean and the other by people of African-Caribbean descent born in the UK.

> There are two different types of Caribbean knowledge ... within the community, because ... the people that came from the West Indies who had some education and knowledge of the West Indies have a completely different perspective than the Afro-Caribbeans that's born in England, and they see a different philosophy, and you have to deal with them differently. (6 April 1995)

He continued:

> ... It's very difficult sometimes to contemplate and actually get to grips with the young people that was born here of Afro-Caribbean parents because their perspective of mind is completely – basically it's not their fault because it's two different upbringings, although we are first and second generation the up-bringing that I had is completely different than the Afro-Caribbeans that are born in England have got. They have a different way of living and they have a different philosophy altogether, completely different, and it's a different job that the other Afro-Caribbeans have. (6 April 1995)

This poses special problems for the continuation of many African-Caribbean organisations. According to a key worker at Leeds Black Elders Association (23 March 1995):

We realise that we cannot go on for ever, and the sensible approach we try to look for successors to get them interested in [our organisation] ... We think that at their age with their energy and drive they could be an asset to the organisation itself. But I'm afraid that they think that we are a bit dull and boring. ... Even on occasions when we get the odd individual they don't last for very long because our ways of doing things, I suppose [they find] it is very boring. They just don't want to know.

He is aware that this situation has been compounded by rising expectations and the changing economic climate, saying:

It was much more easier for the youths [before the 1970s] because my struggles was to find somewhere to live. Jobs was easier to come by. There was not as much pressure because society was not as advanced as it is and we did not expect as much as this generation expect. The education that I had is completely on a different wavelength [from the education they have]. There is a higher expectation of achieving education standard, achieving material things, ... and that's the great divide. (23 March 1995)

Although as previously argued, the achievement of a higher socio-economic position can sometimes create a further dilemma.

Sometimes you think you have the answer, ... you think you are there but you are not there because at one time we thought, 'just make sure that all the Black people that born up here have a good education, and everything is aright' – and that's not the case. Education although it gives you a greater perspective, could improve your quality of life, [but] does not guarantee you a higher standard of living. ... We must tell our young people that because you achieve higher education it does not mean that you are going to achieve a higher standard of living – it is a part of the tool to achieve a higher standard of living but it's not everything, it's more diverse. (Education activist, 6 April 1995)

There is a very strong community consensus that not everyone in the African-Caribbean community has succeeded. Those who have achieved success in their chosen area must put something back into the community. Achievers are under a moral imperative. Those who do not assist their less fortunate community sisters and brothers are usually deemed to have 'sold out', and are generally ostracised by the majority of African-Caribbeans. According to one education activist (6 April 1995), African-Caribbean achievers are obligated to ask themselves, *'what can I do for my Black brothers and sisters who have not succeeded?'* He is adamant that helping others spiritually, financially and mentally has to be the *'cornerstone'* of our philosophy, where *'every little bit helps'*.

Lack of support for African-Caribbean businesses

Another important area of concern is the lack of community solidarity or support for African-Caribbean businesses. Some African-Caribbeans shun African-Caribbean stores because they prefer to shop at businesses owned by South Asians or Europeans. According to a business advisor of African-Caribbean descent (20 April 1995):

> We have very little respect for each other really, and I think you will find that some people are not happy to know that their neighbour next door is running a large business and they're not doing anything, they feel envious of that. It's also about the attitude of the same people that you are trying to service. ... In other words the vandalism, the distastefulness that you get from your own kind of people – that you are trying to get rich quick, and who do you think you [are] kind of thing. ... You hear people talking about Black people [that they are] like crabs in a barrel. If one crab tries to climb out the others try to pull it backwards. A lot of these things might be seen as tribal problems in that a lot of us come from Africa, from different tribes, and we stick to these tribes.

In May 1997 similar images were used by Richard Majors in his conference address to one hundred men of African descent at the West Yorkshire Playhouse in Leeds:

> One of the things we do not do in the Black community whether here in Britain or the United States is to show support for each other. ... This lack of support in the Black community is often referred to as crab antics or crabs in the barrel effect. ... You know how crabs will be in a barrel and crabs start moving up to the top of the barrel and then as soon as one almost gets to the top the other little crabs will grab him ... and pull him right back down to the end of the barrel. (Majors in Hylton [ed.], 1997, 11)

Part of the argument for customers and businesses to remain in the confines of the Black community is the concept of the 'black pound'. It is based on a philosophy of self-help and inward investment, urging African-Caribbean consumers to support African and African-Caribbean businesses by using their services or buying their goods. This allows business owners to prosper by becoming strong and financially viable and able to reinvest in the community by creating further jobs. This re-circulation of inward community investment is part of the process of helping to build a strong community, providing role models and assisting African-Caribbeans to respect themselves and so gain the respect of others. According to a business advisor activist (20 April 1995):

> Regeneration for me is people doing different things at different levels and using that money to carry on the whole lot. In other words to reinvest the money, ... and it just keeps going around in that particular area.

This community concept was imported from the USA and has its roots in the traditions of self-help and self-organisation as typified by Marcus Garvey for example and his Universal Negro Improvement Association, and his Black Star Liner operation which he organised to transport diasporan Africans back to the African continent (Sewell, 1987). The concept is also a direct descendent of the self-help initiatives of the 1960s Black Panther Organisations and the past and present schemes advocated by the Nation of Islam in the USA and the UK. Today the issue of the 'black pound' has a strong link to aspects of an Africancentric agenda. This is a reflection of the life-style choices encompassing all aspects of a person's 'being' – the educational, social, spiritual and the economic.

Lack of support for African-Caribbean businesses by some African-Caribbeans can be classified as the remnants of a mentality engendered during three hundred years of transatlantic African slavery. Often termed 'a slave mentality', it has created and sustained group divisions, individualism and competition at the expense of supporting the community. Although community and supportive endeavours were not completely destroyed the legacy of physical and psychological brutality remains. Therefore the recreation of a positive sense of self becomes an urgent issue.

Chapter 2
Creating self-identity

Spirituality

African-Caribbean group formations have a spiritual context although this may not be presented in an overtly religious manner (Hylton, 1997, 10-11). Unpublished research by Wanda Bernard (1995) 'Working with men for change' supports this finding. She used an Africancentric perspective to analyse the survival strategies of a group of African-Canadian and African-Caribbean UK men. Spirituality was a key quality that *'kept them sane'*. Other strategies were personal values and family support, role models, education and marketable skills, setting attainable goals, political and racial consciousness, employment or self-employment and a positive African identity. This present study found strong indications that individuals who are involved in group activities are sure of their purpose, have a strong sense of the justice of their case and the injustices they have endured. The emphases of group actions are geared to set the record straight. Invariably these themes are constructed in light of an Africancentric approach, viewing western concepts as suspect and debilitating to people of African descent who live and work in the western diaspora. These notions are strongly felt, particularly with reference to the maintenance of positive Caribbean/African families. A Rastafarian activist expressed a widely held African-Caribbean view:

> ... basically, values from the host society have been adopted, and ways of being with people. Hostility, that's how they [majority UK community] operate, just general hostility. So it is important for us to instil in our children that we don't have to live like hostile beings, and you have to be careful when you are out there. (London group interview, 25 June 1995)

The African and African-Caribbean approach to individual, family and collective provisions has a strong emphasis on a unified approach towards individual and group life-cycle. This organisational structure is holistic, with emphasis on self-healing individual and collective trauma and pain from outside forces, and overcoming internal potential divisions such as gender, socio-economic position and differing skin tones. The concept of spirituality does not refer particularly to the religious adherence that is a major aspect of many African-Caribbeans' lives. Spirituality refers to religious adherence but also to a particular way of life encompassing strength, perseverance, forgiveness and the ability to build and concentrate on self-knowledge without posing the destruction of, or conflict with other ethnic groups. It is concerned with inner contemplation and outer activities linked with the building of positive individuals and communities. It is concerned with the manner of verbal expression and with knowledge of an alternative history extending beyond Europe. There is an emphasis on knowledge of self and knowledge of others, particularly Europeans. Spirituality is an internal spark generating a power transcending the written word. In contrast, aspects of UK economic liberalism such as competition, the market as a purifying force, hierarchy and differentials, helps to assist the individual to survive life on the outside but does not encourage inner self-development. According to a London (SGI) UK Buddhist of African-Caribbean descent:

> ... there's nothing about sustaining the society; they [majority UK community] are not brought up to think like that, and this is where I feel there is a difference. Because they're brought up for the outside, they're not brought up encouraging things on the inside. It's a very dangerous way. ... It doesn't train you for survival (London group interview, 2 July 1995).

The religious aspect of spirituality is used as a resource to create a sense of calm, inner strength and knowledge. A Seventh Day Adventist views this as:

> A kind of knowledge that whatever may happen to me, I have the resources to overcome it: ... it doesn't mean that everything's going to be fine, but that I'll be able to deal with it (London group interview, 21 May 1995).

'Roots' actions and informal contacts

Another key issue of community groups is their preference for grass-roots activity. In Leeds there is a strong attachment to and preference for self-help and self-organised group types. This is used to create individual and community pride. In this scenario, patronisation is un-welcome, while grass-roots activity is prized. The 'top-down' approach to organisational activity, whether initiated by liberal mem-bers of the majority community or liberal Africans, African-Carib-beans or South Asians, is usually rejected. In Leeds, African-Carib-bean activists and the wider African-Caribbean community have tenuous links with liberal 'race' organisations such as the Commission for Racial Equality (CRE). The actions of such organisations do not enter the consciousness of the majority of Leeds activists or the rank-and-file. Liberal 'race' organisations are considered irrelevant to the everyday struggles of African-Caribbeans, especially when actions or counter-actions have to be rapid and decisive. Organising with neigh-bours, organising the rank-and-file these are the dominant operations of African-Caribbean groups in Leeds. Max Farrar (1988), a well-known socialist activist from the European majority community, made a similar analysis of the politics of Black youth workers in Leeds during the 1970s:

> I argue that we are witnessing in Harehills and Chapeltown the growth of a new form of radical politics, led by sections of the Caribbean community, but involving Asians and white people as well. ... In each of the recent political actions, black youth workers and their friends have taken the initiative. On each occasion, their call for a public meeting has received wide support from the younger members of the Caribbean community, from radical sections of the Asian community, and from white people who live and/or work in the Harehills and Chapeltown neighbourhoods. Several issues stand out. Firstly, they do not rely on the official channels of protest – the police or council liaison committees, or the local Community Relations Councils, or the local office of the Commission for Racial Equality, or the council's Ethnic Minorities Unit or its committees. Nor do they turn to the existing black organisations or their leaders. Their first step is always to mobilise the ordinary people of the neighbourhood. The second step is to form an organisation which specifically deals with the issue at hand, and the organisation is composed of people who volunteer themselves at the public meeting and is responsible to the public meetings. The third step is determined by the organisation established at the meeting. Frequently, the organisation decides to place demands on the relevant agencies. (Farrar, 1988, 110)

Although group activity starts from the local, all the activists interviewed in Leeds adopted a national or international focus as a part of their organisational activities.

I network a lot so I have lots and lots of contact[s] up and down the country (Education activist, 9 February 1995).

Added to this was an Africancentric approach, which was present to a varying extent. They are also motivated by Christian ideals, and one key activist arrived at an African/Black nationalism from his deep-seated trade union and socialist industrial background. As would be expected from individuals at the forefront of activity, all have a positive sense of self, and being of African descent, they all wanted to build a strong African-Caribbean community in Leeds as part of creating a strong African community in the diaspora. The Leeds activists' openness to outside ideas is built on their theoretical positions – they view African-Caribbeans as linked in time and space. They recognise connections with past events and ongoing ideas and actions in Africa, the Caribbean, USA and all areas of African and African-Caribbean settlement in the UK. Their ideas are compounded by their extensive travel experiences. They have travelled widely in the UK, Europe, the Caribbean and Africa. Those who were born outside Leeds were involved in organisations before they settled in Leeds. In reality their political and organisational skills were honed outside Leeds in areas such as Coventry, Liverpool and London. Some had acquired their skills in, for instance, Barbados, St Kitts and Nevis, Jamaica, Ghana, Sierra Leone, Guinea, the Gambia or Liberia.

These activists are aware of cultural and political events outside the Leeds area. One education and arts activist (5 February 1995), for example, was informed about London based groups such as the Black Lawyers Association, the National Black Caucus and various educational and other solidarity and cultural groups. He read a selection of Black national newspapers including the *Caribbean Times* and *The Voice*. Information gleaned from national events informs his local organisational strategies in cultural groups encompassing education, arts and music issues. Another activist involved in education (9 February 1995) is particularly strong on her awareness of events and groups in Birmingham's Handsworth district (a mental health project, Marcus Garvey Nursery, training organisations, a Black school and

Carnival committee). She is also aware of African-Caribbean activities in Nottingham and mental health schemes in London. Some activists have contacts with African, African-Caribbean and other groups outside Leeds. However, in most instances these contacts are personal rather than formal and are not organised through the groups with which they are associated.

Contacts between African-Caribbean groups in Leeds are much like those elsewhere. Contact and co-operation are usually due to informal friendships and links between the activists in various groups rather than through written or formal ties. National group co-operation tends to mirror the kind of co-operation occurring at the local level. In Leeds the links African-Caribbean organisations maintain with national or other African-Caribbean groups in other UK cities are a reflection of the loose, informal local organisational contacts that predominate. For example, the key activist involved in the Chapeltown Independent After School has maintained long term contacts with many local key activists in Leeds' African-Caribbean community. After School activists are involved in a variety of other groups and organisations such as Assegai, the Afrikan Curriculum Development Association, Black Governors Information Network, Leeds Barbados Association, Leeds Black Elders Association, the Mandela Centre management committee and the People's Arts Council. All these links with the After School are through friendship, personal or political ties, without the formality that would require written formulae of duties, rights and reciprocal arrangements. Before it was formed in 1987, After School personnel had already made informal links with existing supplementary schools in Leeds, London and Liverpool but these are tenuous and many have not been cultivated. The example of the After School is typical of individual and group interactions and links. An analysis of other African-Caribbean groups in Leeds will produce a similar typology of informal contacts and inter-group connections, particularly with local African-Caribbean organisations. This does not imply that there is no competition between groups. For instance, there is slight tension between local community radio stations and performing and visual artists, mainly over the influence and power of community DJs, especially with regard to the music content of programmes concentrating on sex and violence. An arts and education activist (20 February 1995) expresses it thus:

> My biggest fight is against the musicians ... because we live in a town where because we have had to talk to ourselves so much ... we can't sort things out, music has been the easiest way to do this. Also because of communication powers it's very easy to listen to, you don't have to go anywhere, everybody has a radio in the house even if you don't have a cassette or record player, and there are pirate stations. Also the radio station has become like a religion. Who says that 'religion is the opium of the people?' – Karl Marx. Music has become the opium of the people. For instance if you try and discuss religion with the kids or even adults they'll say – 'I believe in God, bla! bla! bla', and then you think they don't go to church, where're they getting this from, and then you realise it's the music. In particular most of it has a high amount of gospel and scripture, moral, Bob Marley, ... all these people. So in a sense they're getting their religion from the music, but what is it doing? Because they're getting everything else from this music as well, including high sex, high pornography, high violence, everything cancels itself out so they still end up with nothing. But what happens, the people who have been running this music thing around the town for so long are well insitued and they are what you might call the de facto bosses of the town. They are the bosses, the Mafia bosses if you like, of the town. So all this big fight, I'm fighting literally against music.

Informal contact arrangements can be a workable way of getting results as and when help and assistance are required. Such loose structural arrangements effectively correspond with the loose structure of most of the voluntary African-Caribbean agencies in Leeds, and are in tune with a wider African-Caribbean ethos: a relaxed atmosphere for public and private affairs. Formalities are felt to stifle creativity and mutual bonds of affection. These feelings have deep historical significance where excessive structure and rigidity ('a stiff upper lip') can be classified as a signifier of neo-European or neo-English allegiance. It is not the African way. African-Caribbean individuals who appear to revel in rigid adherence to structures of bureaucracy risk being labelled 'English' – a label most Leeds African-Caribbean activists want to avoid.

In 1988 a local cultural and political commentator and activist from the majority community observed how the radical loose organisational structures existing in the African-Caribbean community in Leeds created problems for many socialist activists from the majority community.

> Only rarely do the young black activists make reference to the traditional languages and methods of socialism or communism, even in the forms expounded by the major black radical writers. On the other hand, a radical, political language is being developed in myriad forms, ranging from the voices on pirate radios, microphone operators at sound systems and independent recordings, to arguments and discussions at community education classes, conferences and political meetings. This break in the language of socialism poses a problem for those white radicals who can only recognise socialist tendencies when they conform to the prescriptions of their own heroes, but it is time that this is recognised as a problem for the politics of socialism as traditionally defined, rather than as a problem for the progressive people of the inner cities. It seems to me that the radical political language being forged by the young black workers and their supporters in Harehills and Chapeltown makes an advance on traditional socialism in one important respect: it contains within it existential and spiritual concepts which have been almost excluded from modern left-wing politics. Starting from concerns with equal rights and justice, and including references to the international oppression of the black peoples of the diaspora, this language often focuses on the 'dread' personal experience and the need to transcend spiritual as well as material oppression (Farrar, 1988, 112).

Farrar acknowledged that he had some reservations concerning the effectiveness of *'operating with a very loose structure'* but he recognised its power to organise at the *'grass-roots'*. He acknowledged that even in loose structural arrangements, structures can be found.

> Their critique of hierarchy and the commitment to remaining organic to their communities has already been mentioned, and these, combined with tactical requirements make for an acceptance of the obvious deficiencies of operating with a very loose structure. These deficiencies are often overcome by the close personal networks that operate within the communities, but there are many occasions on which they are not, and until genuinely democratic organisational procedures are developed, these problems will remain. It has to be remembered, however, that conventional socialist organisations can claim very little for their internal democracy and even less for their ability to mobilise people in support of their conception of the 'cause', so while the 'tyranny of structurelessness' may sometimes operate within these campaigns, this has to be offset against their undoubted ability to take effective action over a wide range of issues. This ability

is itself an indication that there is more structure and organisation here than a casual observer would recognise. (Farrar, 1988, 113-114)

Importantly, this loose organisational structure does not entail poor commitment to group aims by their members. Also, when links are made in the heat of group formation and debate, speedy community responses are developed. This was exemplified by activities after police actions outside the Chapeltown Young People's 10-2 Club in 1994, when youths were attacked and arrested by the police. Links were quickly established with the London-based National Black Caucus, and a speaker was invited to the fledgling Black Direct Action meeting. He became a key member of the defence committee, which issued leaflets and organised an impressive protest march on 16 December 1994, and was a leading participants in maintaining the call and response slogans chanted by the marchers. This support was officially acknowledged in the first newsletter produced by Black Direct Action, in November 1994:

The Campaign Committee and Members of the Community would like to acknowledge the tremendous help and support given by both local and national individuals and organisations, particularly the National Black Caucus, without whose help and advice the Campaign would not have been so speedily organised, and who advised and assisted the Campaign Committee with policing Chapeltown on Bonfire Night.

The link between the Leeds activists and the Caucus extends back to 1975. The Black Caucus assisted Leeds youths after police attacked them during bonfire night celebrations. Tensions between the police and African-Caribbean youths had been building up, particularly after the police attempted to stop the celebrations. According to Farrar (1988, 100):

On 5th November 1975 around 100 youths threw bricks at police cars patrolling the Bonfire Night festivities on Spencer Place in Chapeltown. During the course of a two or three hour running battle, five policemen were injured, two extremely seriously, and several police cars were smashed up.

Between these occasions in 1979 and 1994, the Caucus had no official links with youth organisations in Leeds. What existed were loose friendly informal contact arrangements based on shared experiences and political imperatives to provide assistance when required. Such rank and file activities, although linked to wider issues, are constructed out of group identity created through a notion of sharing spatial location. Invariably the creation of such a community has to have boundaries, and decisions concerning outsiders have to be made.

Defence of urban space

For social movements theorists such as Castells (1983) and Gilroy (1987), group actions, particularly urban actions, are focused on the renegotiation of urban space as means of defending cultural identity organised around territory. This thesis can be upheld by examining where groups are located, who is involved or excluded from them, and the theoretical and practical organisational methods they adopt. By all three criteria, African-Caribbean groups are outside the existing class-based categories of theorists such as Mandel (1977), Mann (1973) and Parkin (1971), who studied group actions organised in the workplace or public spheres of activity. African-Caribbean self-organised groups have a local focus – although they may consider themselves part of loosely structured national or international networks. Unlike other social movements such as women's liberation organisations, anti-nuclear protesters and ecology groups, individuals who form African-Caribbean community self-organised groups are concentrated in local area actions because of racism and social exclusion, rather than operating as a body of spatially dispersed individuals who come together periodically to form a large group bound by their theoretical beliefs. Leeds African-Caribbean group activists live together in a small confined space surrounded by larger city spaces occupied by individuals and groups who can be wholly unsupportive to African-Caribbean individual and group objectives. Defence of space can mean the physical defence of the area where members of the group reside, work and organise – an attempt to hold ground when there seems to be nowhere else to go. According to an education activist (9 February 1995):

> ... some people – African-Caribbean people – say that they wouldn't move out [of Chapeltown] because this is where they live, and they have lived there for many years, and they love it, and they think it's wonderful even with all the problems they have to face, and even though they might admit they wouldn't want to go out late at night on their own and walk down the streets or something like that. On the

other hand there are people who said that they would like to get out of here because of those problems, and others have mentioned people who have moved into more white areas and come back because they felt isolated.

There may also be fears lest defeat and loss of ground might lead to dispersal of the community and so weaken its cohesion. Few would deny that the Chapeltown area lacks amenities such as cafeterias, African-Caribbean owned businesses or permanent arts spaces. An arts and education activist (20 February 1995) expresses the general concern:

I would say that in Chapeltown you have got a higher percentage of people with artistic expression, or potential artistic (expression) than anywhere else, maybe even more so than other areas where there are more Black people in a much larger area. ... We don't have a theatre space in Chapeltown – the West Yorkshire Playhouse is spending money to get us to go down there. We are saying, 'all we need is a one room' – if we can develop our own little place then we will happily go and perform, but we keep having to go to perform in your space surrounded by people who haven't got much sympathy or under-standing with what we do. But if we can practice our little art up here [in Chapeltown], when we perfect it we can take it elsewhere.

Yet, Chapeltown is a visually attractive area with large handsome Victorian houses surrounded by new housing developments con-structed by various housing associations. With its wide roads and public parks, it was once a middle class haven, laid out and built on hills three miles from the city centre. Anecdotal evidence suggests that defence of this space is linked to underlying unease among its African-Caribbean residents about an unspoken project to reclaim the area for the upwardly mobile European middle classes. It may be in the interest of some people to cultivate a bad reputation for Chapeltown to preci-pitate mass relocation to other areas in an effort to escape the negative tag currently attributed to its residents. There is some outward move-ment, although some people who moved into mainly white areas felt isolated and returned to Chapeltown. The majority of the local African-Caribbean community remain resolute and stay in the area. A 62 year old woman who came to the UK and Leeds during the 1960s is typical:

A lot of people don't want to say they live in Chapeltown because it is a red light district – but I am never afraid to say that's where I live. ... From I came to England I came into Chapeltown. ... Lots of people think bad about it and don't like to say that they live there, but it is my community, that's where I am and that's where I stay. I never had contact with any of the muggers – the people around here Black or white are the same really. I go to church but when I come back I have to make well of everyone (28 January 1993).

In private discussions with Leeds activists and in formal interview situations I found that African-Caribbeans in Leeds were referred to as in some way 'backward'. According to an African born education and arts activist who has travelled and worked in Africa, the Caribbean, Europe and the USA:

... this community is the slowest community that I have ever been in, in terms of group dynamics, group awareness, solidarity [and] the discussion of problems (5 February 1995).

This is partly provoked by the lack of welcome extended to outsider activists not born or long resident in Leeds. I have reported how the ideas and actions of outsider activists may be treated with suspicion or total rejection. There is a contradiction between failing to welcome activists and ideas from outside Leeds and the need to connect with the issues, debates and solutions achieved nationally and internationally by people of African descent. Rejection here is built on the premise that the outsider is unable to contribute worthwhile productive ideas or actions to assist African-Caribbean struggles in Leeds. Outsider activists are thought to lack the understanding of the particular history and dynamics of the local African-Caribbean community in Leeds. Outsiders cannot be trusted because the nature of their true commitment to progressive African-Caribbean struggles is unknown and must therefore be treated with caution. They might be spies, they might be police informers, they might wish to collect information and insights for their own gratification or personal career advancement. In all these potential scenarios the African-Caribbean community would be used without accruing benefit outcomes. In this paradigm of beliefs the outsider is considered a potential threat. Rejection of the outsider is a method of survival – the onus is put on newcomers to prove their credentials, to show by word and deed that they are concerned about the best interests of the wider community and will not initiate actions which might be detrimental to the community project. Judgement is reserved not because of personal individual threat but because of the possibility of harm to the community as a whole. Reserving judgement is a collective response, intended to safeguard the wider interests of local friends and neighbours. It could be classified as a group survival tactic. Outsiders might also present a dilemma created by the informal and close-knit methods used for group organising where activities occur in a small area with a village atmosphere. According to an arts and education activist (20 February 1995):

> We live in a large African society in Chapeltown, so if you like, there is not a lot of call for me to do other than work amongst the people [Africans and African-Caribbeans] who I work with.

Many people make connections and comparisons between Chapel-town and Harehills areas and 'easy-going' parishes in Jamaica, Barbados and St Kitts. Although there are tensions that lead some individuals to avoid actively advertising that they reside in Chapeltown or Harehills, many others are positive about the areas they sometimes refer to as little Jamaica or little Barbados. According to a male Chapeltown resident who has lived in the UK for 36 years:

> I would not change and live anywhere else, it is like Jamaica (February 1993).

Some local people can recognise the children of particular families simply by their physical appearance. Family names are sometimes used as a method of locating individuals in a spatial continuum where specific names can have resonance, especially where members of particular families are or have been respected community activists. This is the approach to community cohesion still to be found in Africa and the Caribbean, and which to some extent has been carried to the close spatial networks in UK cities. Practically all individual actions, whether good, bad or indifferent, will eventually emerge to circulate in the Leeds African-Caribbean community, and will contribute to the historical mix forming a part of the individual's family lineage. In this environment, group organisations are created not with strangers but usually with people who know each other – neighbours, work colleagues, or ex-school and unemployed friends. So although not all actors are physically acquainted with fellow activists their names or deeds would be known – it would be public or community property.

There is always a thin link or connection to each actor so the actual and potential for mutual understanding, friendships or enmity is ever present. Meetings take place at communal venues such as community centres, school premises, business and training centres and church halls, but more often in activists' homes. People meet not only to plan and execute group actions but also for social reasons, although the two are sometimes combined. Unlike group activities in cities with larger and more dispersed African-Caribbean community groups, activities in Leeds invariably draw the activist into close personal relationships with colleagues who may know each other intimately. Perhaps it is not surprising that such organisational forms do not always readily accept new members into their ranks.

Castells (1983) and Gilroy's (1987) concepts of defence of urban space have been useful analytical tools in this study but they do not take into account that not all people with the same ethnicity will gel or have the same aims. Their age range, gender and religious affiliations also count, and so does whether individuals are insider or outsider activists. Some Leeds activists consider the rejection of new activists as parochial behaviour. African-Caribbeans in Leeds are sometimes considered as 'cut off' or disconnected from the radicalism evident in larger UK cities, notably London. It is widely debated among the Leeds activists that African-Caribbeans in Leeds are more difficult to motivate to action than those in larger inner city areas. They also tend to accept many situations which their counterparts in other cities would reject, and are prone to in-fighting, so reducing the spread of radical organisational forms. For instance there is a gender divide according to which men are excluded and seen as *drug runners, ... all men are not to be dealt with in a positive way*. The same interviewee noted another division:

> The negatives about Africans, ... there is also the problem of under-representation of Africans in the community at all levels. Under-representation of Africans from the continent in activities to do with Carnival for example, to do with institutional roles. ... Everything is cornered off.' (Education and arts activist, 5 February 1995)

The criticism most often heard concerns the belief that they are an 'island' – the notion that African-Caribbeans in Leeds seem to believe the relatively small area of Chapeltown and Harehills where they reside in significant numbers to be the centre of the world, maybe the symbolic centre of the universe. One education activist, although apprehensive lest this defence of space was geared to the exclusion of ideas and actions from outsider activists, did not argue against these feelings.

> What I am saying is if you are going to argue about being together, do something positive, don't sit there and spout all this history because we're making history today, and we have to go back and come forward, and we have to evaluate, and we have to assess and move on. But don't just keep going back and say we did this we did that, move on – try to move on. Look at what there is, what needs to be done, and more people get up and do something. Whereas what I found is there is a small group of very active people who will just burn out eventually if others don't stop talking and do something. (9 February 1995)

If there is some truth in these assertions, one could argue that such an insular approach can sometimes be a great source of strength, aiding the spread of a communal response to events such as physical attacks from the police or the creation of formal associations. Two examples of speedy defensive response by African-Caribbean youths to police attacks were the bonfire night battles with the police in 1975, and the Chapeltown Young People's 10-2 Club incident in October 1994. More formalised group responses are evident in educational attainment and in further and higher education and Access provision. These include (a) the formation at a public meeting in 1973 of the Chapeltown Parents Action Group, which organised a successful campaign against racism and poor educational resources at Earl Cowper Middle School in Chapeltown, and (b) the formation of the group known as Assegai, from delegates at a locally organised education conference, 'Black Education Now', in June 1994. Assegai's aims were to network with other African-Caribbean education groups in Leeds to improve the sharing of information and thus enhance effectiveness.

Parochial beliefs can be a source of weakness because of the tendency to reduce the world to the local. It is argued (Castells, 1983) that activists who feel unable to control or have an effect on wider issues withdraw to the local as a shelter where they feel in control of their destinies. In this situation it can be difficult or impossible to make links with other people in similar situations and learn from their successes and failures. Such sharing prevents the recurrence of unsuccessful actions. Parochialism is opposed to the idea, understanding and recognition of wider unity, although such an intense focus can be used as a mobiliser of local community actions with an emphasis on reactive defensive measures incorporating self-definition, cultural affirmation and reflexivity.

Social exclusion and self-reflexivity

Coming to terms with self can be a difficult process. Africans and African-Caribbeans can often pinpoint significant moments in their lives that make them aware of the complexities of having African or African-Caribbean heritage and living in a European environment. Cultural and religious differences may appear unimportant – until it becomes evident in certain situations, say, education or employment, that they are not being treated equally to Europeans. Then they have to either accept the barriers or try to overcome them. If they accept inequality they need not question the status quo but overcoming it demands that they learn new skills to acquire an appreciation of their African heritage. For example, in the 1930s one woman born in the UK of a European mother and an African-Caribbean UK-born father had her world view shaped by long term involvement with a group of African and African-Caribbean Buddhists.

> I never knew that I was any different to anybody else until ... my mother was a bit of a fighter, and you can imagine being white and marrying a Black at that time. There was a terrible case going on in America about the seven Scottsborough boys, young boys 13-17 accused of raping a white woman, and they were going to be hung and lynched. ... I knew what the difference between Black and white was then. But once I knew the difference between Black and white and I started to go into the history then I didn't want to know anything about whites. But my mother, I was from her womb, you know what can you do? But I am an African, I've got nappy hair, I've got brown skin. I'm not Indian, I'm not an English woman, I'm a world citizen but I am an African and I can't see myself as anything else. ... Africans have laughed at me, joked with me, encouraged me in my beliefs and faiths, but no one will make me waver, that is what I am and that is how I see myself. (Seventy-three year old woman, in London group interview, 2 July 1995)

Another woman began to reassess her situation after she was rejected for a job when her European friend was successful. Both her parents are Africans.

> I was educated here, born here, ... at 14 I tried to get a job. ... I went with a white friend and she got the job and I didn't. You know they said there wasn't any work. So now it was slowly coming to me that I was different, but up until then I sailed through totally unaware, playing with white and Black friends, no problem. (London group interview, 2 July 1995)

Other people have an undaunted commitment to a positive non-European (Caribbean nationalism) self-reference, irrespective of their place of birth. According to one woman, a Seventh Day Adventist in her mid 40s:

> I just see myself as a Grenadian, strange combination. I have got a mixture of African, native Indian and distant European background, so I strongly call myself a Grenadian. ... My niece and nephew have been to Grenada and we are strongly Caribbean. I am West Indian because of my philosophy and my historical sense of being, and we relate to the Caribbean as home. Even though my sisters and my brother were born here they're very much Caribbean. (London group interview, 21 May 1995)

A woman born in Grenada indicated that she had nurtured in her three UK-born boys a strong attachment to Grenada and its culture. This Caribbean island identity has been continued to her four year old granddaughter.

> Well, I never allow them [her three children] to call themselves British – seriously. I suppose they would see themselves as Grenadians born in England, or something. ... Because I don't allow them to see anything else, because I just bombard them with everything Grenadian and West Indian. So if you ask them they will talk about Grenada with the same passion as I do. ... My granddaughter, who's four, has just come back [from Grenada] ... and she will talk with a Grenadian accent. (London group interview, 21 May 1995)

A Leeds arts and education activist is sceptical about how deeply Africancentric or Caribbean people can become while Africans and African-Caribbeans are physically located in the UK or elsewhere in the western diaspora.

> We define ourselves in terms of our environment and no matter how much the sun shines in Chapeltown we still live in England. Because

we speak English we are English, and this is what we tend to forget. Because we speak English we are English, we think English. (20 February 1995)

He is a deeply Africancentric person and his ideas are typical of those who consider physical return to the African continent as essential for African-Caribbeans and other Africans in the diaspora. He cannot agree with people who view emotional return linked to Africancentric knowledge and actions as sufficient. Although this activist works steadfastly to alleviate the present problems of African-Caribbeans and Africans in the UK, particularly in relation to youth and the arts, he strongly favours actual return to Africa as the only lasting solution to providing Africans of the diaspora with emotional and practical peace. These debates have a long history. One high profile Rastafarian activist called Jah Bones (1985, 13) relates how:

> On the 21st of March 1878, a black man Martin R. Delany, who had studied at the Harvard Medical School, presided at the Charleston ceremony to consecrate a ship that would carry several hundred volunteer Afro-American settlers to Liberia. At the turn of the century to the first World War there was a great enthusiasm and organisation by 'radical free' blacks for repatriation to Africa to establish black settler colonies.

This philosophy was upheld by African nationalists such as Marcus Garvey, who by the early twentieth century had built an African nationalist movement called the Universal Negro Improvement Association (UNIA). By 1922 the association could claim to represent the aspirations of seven million members scattered in the USA, the Caribbean, South America, the UK and Africa (Bones, 1985, 13). Today this linear historical line of actions, deep feelings and expressions towards spiritual and practical reconnection with Africa, particularly areas of the west coast, ancient Egypt and Ethiopia, are still very much alive. Jah Bones (1985, 70) expresses these hopes and feelings thus:

> The experience of being drawn to Africa is something else. It puts one in a situation where one finds oneself constantly thinking, talking, walking and acting African. To the Rasta, most definitely, Africa is no myth; it is the biggest reality that he experiences. It does not matter that the average Rasta does not know Africa, in a physical sense. What really matters is that the average Rasta knows, only too well, Africa in the spiritual and psychological terms. To Rasta this is very

important because those who had profited from our slavery and colonisation have tried to kill this knowledge. The fact that they have not succeeded scores well among I n I. That proved, as it were, that Africa is real and that repatriation is inevitable.

The issue of physical or philosophical return to Africa is linked to the notion that individuals absorb the cultures surrounding them; that individuals are a reflection of the cultures and the language/s they speak. This is evident to people who learn another language, where successful understanding requires knowledge of the new culture and creative thoughts within its parameters. This has been the spur for some African-Caribbeans and African-Americans to change their European names to African names, to wear African clothes and to learn the rudiments of at least one African language such as Swahili or Yuruba. The need to retain a strong concept of Caribbean and African identities is based on the notion that negation of these identities will eventually render individuals and their community powerless. This scenario is most evident when individuals are rejected by sections of UK society, when they have nowhere else to go and nowhere to turn for self-gratification. There is an understanding that individuals require positive identities to enable them to counter racism.

Africancentric ideas present an alternative view of history and counter ideologies. These theories reject notions of individual struggle where survival is at the expense of others and where power is regarded as a zero sum formation so that only a finite amount of it is available. This engenders competition where 'I' try to grab the major share at the expense of 'them'. On the contrary, African nationalism and African-centric themes are concerned with co-operation, not competition. Afrocentricity tries to balance the concepts of individuality with the needs and functions of family and community ideals and commitments. The ideas are based on co-operation and understanding of individuals linked in time and space to a greater whole. It is only the healthy continuance of the greater whole (family and community) that provides the foundation from which individuals can emerge (Browder, 1989; Asante, 1988). Anything tending to undermine the-group will therefore undermine the individual. Racism and aspects of UK liberalism which stress the merits of the isolated individual in free competition are undermining. This rejection of competition is expressed when activists consult with other activists and groups before taking actions on behalf of the community as a whole, or when they urge groups to combine their resources to improve the efficiency and strength of the Black voluntary sector by not competing for funding. Not competing is a key perspective of Africancentric ideas that challenge the divide and rule strategies that have been so successful a part of the colonial policies of control used against Africans and other non-Europeans. Accordingly, the rejection of competition between African-Caribbean individuals and groups can be viewed as a rejection of a new colonialism based on access to finances and political power. When African-Caribbeans reject competition and replace it with co-operation they link with fellow Africans and African-Caribbeans who are combating similar structures and forces as an act of self-healing.

There are usually positive reasons why groups form, and invariably the reasons are to do with the solving of practical issues. To arrive at a solution that can be of use in the future requires knowledge of self and knowledge of an alternative history. These themes are mediated through the concept of spirituality. There is a sense of African-Caribbeans in the diaspora struggling with the dilemma of their recent past. Their story is either not told truthfully or not told at all – is in fact hidden from history. In each area of the lives of African-Caribbeans, whether in education, art, religion, the family, organisational structures, music, dance or sporting prowess, the issues to overcome are invariably wider than the immediate problem. They are linked to culture and historical debates concerning the correct mode of survival or adaptation to the west. This is what Goulbourne (1993, 183) has described as the dilemma of taking part in UK society while at the same time withdrawing and trying to change certain elements and structures detrimental to African-Caribbean individual and collective self-worth. The struggles are played out on two fronts. The first deals with external individual and collective forces that seek to destroy the very being and essence of African-Caribbean people – the explicit and implicit actions from sections of the majority community. The second dilemma deals with internal forces such as individual and communal issues, ideas and actions which stem from within the African-Caribbean community. The interpersonal actions of African-Caribbean gender debates fit this agenda precisely. These arguments are developed in Chapter 3.

Self-healing is concerned with knowledge of self and history, creation of unity, and providing practical and theoretical tools that solve existing problems and enable further issues to be tackled. Healing aspects of African-Caribbean groups are therefore important for current situations and also form key elements for the future, especially if the coping strategies are ultimately internalised by young people. The strategies provide individuals with the strength to withstand the negative external forces without cracking or becoming self-destructive. They acquire the strength to hold on while they also make the required changes to structures and practices. It is important to withstand, to be able to hold on with dignity – to survive. This is not to advocate passivity; it is not suggesting that ideals and hope be surrendered; it is about not going mad or allowing negative issues to adversely affect physical or psychological states. Individuals and groups acquire the tools they need to be able to hold on and eventually to change self and structures. These characteristics are what contributes to the process of self-healing. Physical and mental strength are used in a positive manner. Many African-Caribbean groups have these aspects in their organisational structures.

African-Caribbeans are highly critical of the actions of individuals outside of their community. Scepticism is a major aspect of the African-Caribbean survival armoury. They are equally critical of themselves, although this critique is shared between self and others. They examine self or individual ideas and actions, the 'I', and also the ideas and actions of others in the community, the 'them'. So there will be situations where they perceive themselves to be right, or in possession of the moral high ground because others are in the wrong. *They*, the others, are individuals who make it difficult for the community to survive, to organise, to fight back or to maintain and build communal organisations. Their management committee members might refuse to give up power. *They* are outsiders, informers, and African-Caribbeans who do not support African-Caribbean businesses. Or they may belong to other African-Caribbean groups who perform similar tasks and are therefore regarded as competitors. *They* could be young people who have lost respect for their parents, the community and themselves. A 40 year old Africancentric Leeds youth activist (15 May 1995) commented on the much debated changed ethos of some African-Caribbean youths he encounters:

> It's changed in terms of cohesiveness of the community. When I was growing up there was a certain respect for older Black people, for Black people's property. But nowadays it seems that all the respect is gone. The young people are stealing from their own parents, and when you start stealing from your own parents that means that you can steal from anybody. The trust, the cohesiveness, to me, has gone. ... When I was growing up people older than myself could reprimand me for doing something out of order, and in a sense it instilled a sense of discipline and respect within you. To me, it made me and a lot of other people, better people. But nowadays all that respect is gone.

Self-healing is a major element in any scheme trying to retain the progressive, to retain feelings of being wary while not allowing the process of critique to be taken to extremes. Hearts and minds require healing. In all African-Caribbean groups this concept of self-healing is an important element. It is about the issue of trust and hope enabling the changed process to be of lasting worth. Hence the notions of sisterhood, brotherhood or cousins linked in time and space to cultures and histories rooted in Africa. This can be illustrated by (a) the use of African names for organisations, and the individuals who change their Anglo names to African names. Acquiring an African name has progressed since Malcolm X used the 'X' to signify his lost ancestry that could not be renamed or reclaimed. Parents of African-Caribbean descent are increasingly giving their children African names in a traditional African naming ceremony. I know of four such naming ceremonies in Leeds between 1994 and 1996. Self-healing also entails (b) the need to support African-Caribbean businesses, (c) the need to welcome outsider activists, (d) the need for African-Caribbean groups to work together rather than in competition, and (e) the need to heal African-Caribbean internal community tensions and divisions.

All these issues are aspects of a critique of ideas and actions that emphasise the need to change and adjust. It is understood that there are strong forces at work which in practical terms mean that individuals can be apprehensive of one another. Taken to its extreme it may be judged as self-hate. The majority of African-Caribbeans and certainly the activists I interviewed are keenly aware of these difficult issues and have adopted strategies in their efforts to overcome them. Unless African-Caribbean individuals can address these interpersonal tensions, progress will be retarded or cease. African-Caribbeans are also aware that public policy cannot solve these issues. Most researchers and policy makers are either unaware or do not wish to confront such internal debates because policy issues in the area of visual minority life-chances are usually cast in simple terms (black or white) – although real lives are always more complicated. A perfect example of this is the urgent need for funding bodies to support African-Caribbean groups and researchers involved in the ongoing African-Caribbean inter-personal gender debate. But funding bodies do not understand the essence of the new strategies emerging in the African-Caribbean community and divert monies to issues such as disaffected youth instead of tackling the long term issues. Women need and want mutual respect and emotional support from their partners. Their demands are exacerbated by the effects of racism and social exclusion, which tend to push African-Caribbean men towards the margins of UK society. There are other possible internal divisions which are socio-economic in character.

Internal stratification

Arguments concerning internal stratification are similar to notions about class or socio-economic positions which posit individual or group actions as directly related to the social position the individual or group attains in the structures of a given society. Social position is related to educational attainment, financial wealth or work modes where credit is assigned to mental occupations and discredit to jobs requiring physical labour. Some people have more to lose than others while some do not need to struggle or oppose the *status quo* because they are the makers of the rules or the major recipients of its benefits. Internal stratification is concerned with the analysis of different interests, different consciousness and different needs to act. In the context of radical peasant actions, rich peasants are more likely to be conservative and although they are a part of the peasant world they will only act in support of their poor peasant cousins when they per-ceive that the peasant way of life and existence is threatened and no differentiation will be made between different peasant groups. In this scenario the rich peasants would be swept aside with poor because what is of importance is that they are all peasants (Wolf, 1987, 370). Middle peasants, who are neither rich nor poor have been classified in contradictory terms as reactionary (Marx and Engles, 1981, 225-226), cautious (Scott, 1976, 25), and as forming the base of revolutionary movements (Wolf, 1969), while the poor peasants are a potentially revolutionary sub-section of the peasant community (Moore, 1974, 455). Rich peasants have to be forced into radical activity – if their life-world is not threatened they are content to be separate, above and imposing in their peasant group. They may operate as overseers or intermediaries between external elites and middle and poor peasants; they may be the self-styled community leaders. Similar to other subordinate groups, middle or poor peasants are not suicidal. When they cannot use regular day-to-day survival strategies such as foot dragging, desertion, feigned ignorance, arson, sabotage, pilfering and flight, they will organise and fight back (Scott, 1985, xvi).

Many instances cited in this book have highlighted that African-Caribbeans in Leeds are not one autonomous block but have various divisions, outlooks and organisational strategies. Similarly, while African-Caribbeans operate to raise individual status this is mediated through actions designed to assist the development of group status. Such an approach can be contrasted with peasants who cannot escape the forces outside their community such as a civil or world war, foreign invasion or struggle for national emancipation from a colonial super power. These actions occur outside their community but never-theless threaten their very existence as peasants. Such an outside force and upheaval has the potential to smash all peasants without making reference to their individual social standing in the wider peasant com-munity – the rich would be killed alongside the poor. This scenario concentrates the minds of all peasants, unifying them to overcome their internal socio-economic differences to resist as one unit. Peasants cannot escape their heritage any more than African-Carib-bean individuals can escape their African heritage, whatever their educational attainment, wealth or social position. Similar to the out-side force that unifies peasant community, racism and social exclusion are the outside forces that unify African-Caribbeans and help to heal internal divisions like gender and socio-economic differences. Regardless of their socio-economic position, African-Caribbean individual and community life are both disrupted by racism, because what is important is their African heritage. There is no hiding place as racism would seek them out, and to some extent although African-Caribbeans of high socio-economic status might have the means to fight back, their real position in UK society is linked to the status of their ethnic group. Therefore it makes sense to raise the status collectively of all African-Caribbeans, thereby raising individual status.

This way of understanding is similar to Melucci (1989), where changing one's self and changing society is considered as the same process because the journey is as important as the destination. In other words, the methods we use to interact with others are of equal importance as the end goals. Individuals cannot arrive at the end of the journey without being changed to some extent by the processes they use to achieve their aims. This belief in the power of process is quite different from the belief that new structures will create changes by forcing individuals to re-examine their ideas and change their behaviour – that after changes to their inner consciousness they would undergo a 'change of heart'. Whereas Melucci believes that where involvement is an ongoing task, individual and collective consciousness proceed together to create structural changes (Melucci, 1989, 205-206).

The next chapter provides the final illustration of these arguments, exploring the rise of UK Black men's forums and the linkage to African-Caribbean gender debates.

Chapter 3

Black men's forums and African-Caribbean gender debates

This chapter highlights the relatively new phenomenon of the rise of Black men's forums in several UK cities and the link to ongoing African-Caribbean gender debates. A young African-Caribbean woman at an education parent support group in London encapsulates a widely held belief in the African-Caribbean community:

> I think that the Black man is being systematically destroyed; society hasn't got a use for the Black man, ... and if it cannot have him as a boy it don't want him as a man. ... Basically it lets a few trickle through, but the majority it stamps on their little necks while they are little kids and refuses to allow them to be men. ... They are taking the men more because the man is the one who plant the seed, if they got our men in prison how are they going to multiply? (*Quotations were first used by Dench, 1996, 114 and 115, but this is a new transcription from the original taped recording of an interview I conducted.*)

The type, method and range of African-Caribbean group actions can be heavily influenced by the outcome of private family decisions made by women and men. While the issues have implicit links with efforts to negotiate female and male relationships and the re-construction of African-Caribbean family life, their effects on communal African-Caribbean organisational forms are not yet fully researched. Although supported by intensive debates and discussions by many African-Caribbean individuals and groups in London, Dudley, Manchester, Birmingham and Leeds, the arguments presented here are not the direct outcome of the construction and reconstruction of group actions. Our focus is on existing individual inter-personal relationships, the impact on family life, and the cumulative potentially negative effects on individual and family choices in the UK. But it is worth bringing a theoretical approach to the impact of the gender debate on

55

African-Caribbean group activities. My direct involvement as researcher and participant in gender debates and forums for men of African descent span five years and include four research projects. During this time I have led and been involved in workshops, individual and group discussions, addressed various conferences and helped to develop the Black Men's Forum in Leeds.

African-Caribbean gender debates have a direct bearing on the reconstruction of communal ideas and actions. Individuals analyse their way of life and how their actions intersect with other family members, their partners and children. The discussions strive to create a new cultural framework, equipping the individual and group to survive into the millennium and beyond. They are a reassessment of the past and a pledge to the future. They are about the mobilisation of the mind and body. The difficulty of maintaining positive individual and group African-Caribbean identities during a process of internal debates, discussions and critique are evident. Private family actions do have an effect on the public outcome of observable events where the private gender debates in families manifest themselves in the methods, scope and range of activities undertaken in the public realm. African-Caribbean women have emerged as the individual 'winners' in their private and public realms of activity in the family home, the workplace and community organisations. This manifests itself not only in their individual success in high status occupations but also in their high involvement in African-Caribbean groups. We will see how this gender anomaly could pose serious long term dangers for both the women and the men. These concerns also encourage men of African descent to come to terms with reality by seeking salvation in their separate male forums.

The ideas and concepts of the debate about the roles of women and men are not widely known outside the African-Caribbean community. The nature of these discussions, the relationship between African-Caribbean people, has emerged from within the community itself. There is now widespread concern that unless tactics can be developed to counteract the growing tensions between the sexes, individual, family and community cohesion could well be irreparably damaged or destroyed by forces in the community, although external factors such as slavery, colonialism and overt and covert racism have helped to shape the legacy of existing African-Caribbean gender relationships in the UK. Many African-Caribbean women and men firmly believe that there is a co-ordinated plan sustained by racist elements in this society to destroy the African-Caribbean family in the UK. The following extracts from a Seventh Day Adventist group interview in London (21 May 1995) indicate the flavour of this widespread belief. The woman activist is in her mid-40s.

> ... you realise how these western societies somehow they are really anti, ... a hatred for Black men, and in my study and research as a Caribbean historian I know where it comes from, ... a slave-owner perception of what we are. ... I've realised that picking up young men on the streets with all the 'Sus' law ... is no different from picking them up from Africa and put them in the ship in a chain, locked them in a dungeon and then shipped them to the islands. It's the same sort of slavery but it's of a different kind, and our young men are really in a dilemma. Because our young men sadly don't have the two parents, or some of them who are very, very young mothers ... can't deal with the situation, ... have not the will to help their sons to cope with the system. So you see a lot of lost young men who can't handle the system, whose parents can't handle it. So they are not necessarily bad because they're the same young men you meet on the islands [in the Caribbean]. If they can be positive and do so well in schools and become prime ministers, doctors, lawyers, the same brain, the same mentality, why are they criminalised here? It's as though the society tried to destroy our Black men. It doesn't matter if you're a professor, banker, lawyer, doctor, there is an agenda, in my perception, to destroy the male species of the Black race because when you do that you destroy the nation, and this is my passion for Black men although they give us hassle and hard times in relationships, but I understand that. ... if you destroy the young men from the start you have destroyed the total fabric of Black families in Britain, and I say that with a passion because I can see it.

The knock-on effect of these actions can lead to the destruction of African-Caribbean community in the UK. This is widely understood in the community as being accomplished in various ways, although the key methods involve overt attacks on African-Caribbean men combined with some support for African-Caribbean women, thereby creating a divided community. African-Caribbean young men are excluded from school, criminalised, diagnosed as schizophrenic, sedated with powerful drugs and classified as 'unemployable'. According to a

Buddhist woman of South African descent based with the Sokka Gakkai International (SGI) UK, in London:

> Black men have been pushed out of this society, and I think – like my brothers – if they didn't group together to form something solid then they would get swallowed up by the society and the lack of esteem that is poured on them. (2 July 1995)

Major and Billson (1992) argue that men of African descent in USA urban environments are forced to adopt a cool masculinity or 'cool pose' as a method of surviving in a restrictive society.

> Some African-American males have channelled their creative energies into the construction of a symbolic universe. Denied access to mainstream avenues of success, they have created their own voice. Unique patterns of speech, walk, and demeanour express the cool pose. This strategic style allows the black male to tip society's imbalanced scales in his favor. Coolness means poise under pressure and the ability to maintain detachment, even during tense encounters. Being cool invigorates a life that would otherwise be degrading and empty. It helps the black male make sense out of his life and get what he wants from others. Cool pose brings a dynamic vitality into the black male's everyday encounters, transforming the mundane into the sublime and making the routine spectacular. (Major and Billson, 1992, 2)

Black male action becomes a performance incorporating pride, strength and control (Major and Billson, 1992, 4). Whereas society undermines Black men it tends to support African-Caribbean women. They are chosen by white male employers in preference to African-Caribbean men. African-Caribbean women have aided their survival by adopting different methods to overcome the various forms of racism they encounter, and to confront it in a different manner. Generally, they do not totally reject the system but try instead to work and support each other to find methods of survival that do not incur the loss of their identity, culture and dignity. They therefore perform better than African-Caribbean males in school, gain qualifications and employment, and are the key activists in African-Caribbean voluntary and campaigning organisations. While trying to survive and hold their families together, they are nevertheless sharply aware of the divisions being created between themselves and African-Caribbean men. An African-Caribbean woman in a parent support group (linked to their children's education) in London, voices a familiar theme.

This conspiracy works in two ways, they're getting the men by the prison system, the mental health system. I feel that they are getting the Black women by the education system. Now this society offers many courses to educate the Black woman, ... now for me this level of conspiracy works by I become so educated that I no longer have any use for a Black man and therefore I will look elsewhere into the other races – and so I may have use for a white man, a European man. So therefore I feel that I have become a educated Black woman, I'm not part of this conspiracy. My Black man is not educated like me [although] I'm still leaving him behind, my education has put me on a level where I can only relate to my white counterparts. (*Quotations were first used by Dench, 1996, 115, but this is a new transcription from the original taped recording of an interview I conducted.*)

Women are keen to discuss the problems and issues with their male colleagues to try and find solutions. In many respects the situation can be described as desperate, although viewed from outside of the African-Caribbean community this may not be apparent. Another issue concerns the nature of public debates. It is very difficult for a community enduring racist pressures to conduct critical discussions about their lifestyles and to be open and honest with themselves while fearing that the discussion issues, process and outcome can be appropriated by outsiders and used against them to support notions of them as deviants, or an underclass with a pathological family lifestyle. This is a key dilemma facing the African-Caribbean community in the UK today. African-Caribbean gender debates and male forums seek to understand the reality of African-Caribbean working class life in the UK. This necessarily encompasses the links with colonialism, slavery and the continuing effects of racism, implicit and explicit. The project is an endeavour to build individual and group self-confidence as a method of reducing and eventually eradicating the aspects of African-Caribbean behaviour that are self-destructive, such as the lack of trust between women and men. Susan Taylor, editor-in-chief of a USA magazine, *Essence* (No 59, November 1992) is clearly aware of the issues:

It must be difficult for Black men to feel valued and strong when each day of their lives, and often in their own communities, they are viewed and reacted to as potentially threatening; when their images are always the bad news on the nightly news; when they've been shut out of any arena that white men want for themselves. ... These days,

whenever I pass young brothers in the street, I affirm their presence –
and I even acknowledge those whom I could easily feel fearful of and
who expect me to distance myself from them the way most people do.
I refuse to be afraid of our children. Instead I smile and nod, 'How're
you doing, young brother'? They seem surprised, almost sad, as they
quietly respond to my greeting.

Culture, individual and group identities, survival and mobilisation
tactics are never static. The African-Caribbean gender debates and
male forums are a reflection of this ongoing process of transition and
community rebuilding. A key feature of the discussions is the concern
to find the correct 'moral' framework for individual and group
regeneration and survival in the UK/African diaspora.

Gender debate meetings
African-Caribbean gender themes have been discussed in conferences
and workshops, some of which are mentioned here. Several meetings
were organised by the Exploring Parenthood Moyenda Project, and
Alarm Promotions host regular discussions at Willesden Green
Library in London. The British African-Caribbean Enterprise Club
(BACE), a social discussion group, held an open meeting in June
1994 entitled 'The Strong Black Woman: An Ally or a Threat to the
Black Male/Family'? The United Male Forum is a voluntary organisation of predominantly African-Caribbean men, based in South
London. They host regular group discussions about issues such as:
Black men in crisis, are Black families a thing of the past, are Black
men lazy, and do Black men support their children? The Forum is
open to women members but the emphasis is *'to promote the development of black men'*. The organisation *'strongly believes that the perception of the black man has to be changed. If not for black men today,
then for our children, our families, and our race as a whole, tomorrow'*
(United Male Forum publicity leaflet, 1994).

A conference on '21st Century African-Caribbean Families' was
organised in Septermber 1998 by the West Indian Organisations' Co-
ordinating Committee at Ducie High School in Manchester. Harry
Goulbourne gave the keynote speech, and workshops followed about
mental health, education, school exclusions, male identity, economic
empowerment, domestic violence and youth homelessness. The West
Indian Family Counselling Service in Leeds held conferences in 1993,

1995 and 1997; the 1995 meeting, 'What a state we are in', being promoted as a *crucial debate on Black family life and culture*. In 1996,
conferences were organised by, among others, youth and community
workers at the Claughton Youth and Community Centre in Dudley;
community workers at Simba Community Centre in Shepherds Bush;
and the Association of Pan African Studies and Initiatives held a
seminar at the Bridge Park Complex in north west London. The main
issues examined the roles of both women and men to find out how
people could best adapt to the changing economic and 'moral' pressures of society. Due attention was paid to the strengths, weaknesses
and support mechanisms of Black family survival. I gave keynote
speeches in Leeds (1997), Dudley and Shepherds Bush, assisted by
community worker Louisa Goldstein Thomson and Darren Johnson
from the National Society for the Prevention of Cruelty to Children
(Simba conference leaflet, August 1996; *The Alarm* 1996, 18-19).

Articles, books, journals and reports

A recent article by Sharon James-Fergus (1997), 'Rebuilding the
African-Caribbean Family in Britain', presents a useful overview of the
issues affecting both women and men. It is part of an Institute of
Community Studies publication which examines differing views about
changing relationships and the sexual divisions of labour. Journal and
newspaper articles targeted to Black publications such as *Diaspora*
(1994) *The Alarm, The Weekly Journal* and popular Black fiction
(Augustus, 1994, Baptise, 1994) expose the debate to a wider Black
audience. Black writers and journalists employed on mainstream
newspapers catering to a mainly white audience have also commented
on various strands of ensuing African-Caribbean gender debates. For
example, Lesley Thomas' (1995) *Sunday Times* article, 'She's gotta
have it all', deals with the supposed rejection of African-Caribbean
men by young African-Caribbean women professionals, because the
men are unable to match the women's earning power, new middle-
class lifestyles and 'moral' codes. Yasmin Alibhai-Brown's (1994)
article in the *Guardian*, 'Call me Daddy', highlights African-Caribbean lone parent mothers and their relationship with their partners.
Herman Ouseley's (1993) article in the *Independent* entitled, 'Young,
single and black', noted that Black men are becoming more involved

in child care, while Richard Ford's article in *The Times*, 21 July 1993, 'Fathers 'touch down' – and flee', highlights African-Caribbean conjugal irresponsibility. The issue discussed in these journals, newspapers and fictional books is the rebuilding of positive African identities in a hostile UK environment of racism and indifference towards African people and their culture. This entails the questioning of African-Caribbean female and male ideas and actions that have internalised mutual negative stereotypical views – of African-Caribbean men as emotionally irresponsible and potential muggers, for instance, and of African-Caribbean women as strong, capable and promiscuous. How far are these gender tensions and actions due to African culture or to the effects of slavery, colonialism and racism or patriarchy in general?

Importantly, these divisions would be more severe were it not for the efforts of the women themselves. They are aware of the short and long term difficulties and dangers of the present gender divisions and have generally tried to support male colleagues and partners, especially where the threat is from without and is blatantly racist. African-Caribbean women's critique of aspects of their lives, specifically their relationships with African-Caribbean male colleagues and partners, take the form of direct constructive debates or confrontations, but their thoughts are geared to positive eventual outcomes that benefit the African-Caribbean community in general and African-Caribbean women in particular, because gender relationships will have to change. Women want these changes to be achieved without damaging other minority or majority ethnic groups or individuals, whether female or male. These ideas are typified by this comment at a Leeds African-Caribbean lone parent women group interview.

> I still want to pull up the Black man – I still want to pull him up beside me, but I have to look to my powers first, and then try to do something about it when I can (3 August 1993).

Women and men: a socio-economic comparison

Black men's forums are a mechanism for men of African descent to pull themselves up beside women of African descent by their own efforts. African-Caribbean women are at the forefront of changes which are creating economic, philosophical and tactical divisions between themselves and their African-Caribbean male colleagues. The key issue is gender but there is also a strong emphasis on the effects such discussions and changes have on the wider African-Caribbean community. The outcome of the debate can be classified as an aspect of community regeneration. Changes are not only to do with individual lifestyle at the expense of community growth. Yes, African-Caribbean women are gaining but they are nevertheless concerned about African-Caribbean men and the wider community including children and grandparents. Women are aware that their individual survival as African-Caribbean women who keep their African culture depends on the survival of all members of the African-Caribbean community.

A greater percentage of men than women are involved in enforced 'leisure' caused by unemployment and under-employment. This is especially significant for young men under twenty-five years old. Over half (51%) are unemployed compared to 41% of African-Caribbean women of the same age (Labour Force Survey, Spring, 1994). Fuelling these statistics are the school exclusion rates for African-Caribbean boys. According to the Department of Education (1992) boys are four times more likely to be excluded from school than girls. Nationally Black children are 2% of the school population but they make-up 8.1% of the children who are excluded from school. Black boys, especially African-Caribbean boys, are considered a threat. They are five to six times more likely to be excluded from school for behaviour such as defending themselves from verbal and physical racist attack by other pupils and teaching staff, for the way they walk or talk, the way they dress, and their hair-styles. They behave like adolescents but because they are Black some of their actions are interpreted by some teachers as more anti-social and they tend not to be given a second chance (Bourne, Bridges and Seale, 1994). This disproportionate exclusion rate is confirmed by recent OFSTED research (Gillborn and Gipps, 1996).

In contrast many African-Caribbean women are economically upwardly mobile, involved in continuing and higher education, confident and assertive and are conspicuously involved in the creation and sustenance of African-Caribbean community groups. In Leeds, for instance, this is particularly evident in groups providing advice and advocacy in education, counselling services, health advice and support, religion and other social issues. This is besides their involvement in groups offering support specifically for women, including the Chapeltown Black Writers Group, Barbados Women's Group, Black Lesbian Support Group, Black Women in Europe Network, Leeds Black Women's Forum and Sahara Black Women's Refuge. In contrast African-Caribbean men are struggling to come to terms with their enforced 'leisure' time.

Culture, individual and group identities, survival and mobilisation tactics are in a constant state of flux. It is slowly being acknowledged by some policy makers, family practitioners, and social researchers that the shift in family, social and economic relationships during the past twenty years now require investigation and possible support mechanisms to cater specifically for men. It has been argued that men or the concept of maleness has posed a problem for all societies, and especially the transition from boyhood into adulthood (Dench, 1996). The goal is to find a valued but different place in family life and the wider society. Some of the issues for African-Caribbean men to consider include making and sustaining relationships with girls and women, fathering outside marriage, unemployment, racism, social exclusion, and ways to express personal feelings individually and collectively. The changes occurring in UK society today seem not to have assisted the intricate transition into manhood; on the contrary they may have placed greater stresses on the already frail concept of maleness.

Several changes occurring during the past two decades have had profound effects on both women and men, such as the rise since the late 1960s of white and Black feminist ideas and actions, the changes in access to education and employment, and the restructuring of interpersonal gender relationships including marriage, remarriage, lone parenthood, relationships outside marriage, and the renegotiation of child care and housework. These forces have intellectually and physically altered the way we conduct our lives. New structures are erected and existing relationships renegotiated. While these changes have affected all people in the UK to some degree, change has been most stark for those low on the socio-economic spectrum. This is truest of all for people from the visual minorities, with those of African-Caribbean origin (particularly men) at the forefront of these pressures and changes. Unemployment and under-employment have exacerbate matters by adding the variable of free time with minimal finances.

While African-Caribbean men are trying to cope successfully with the onslaught of economic and cultural changes to UK society, various studies point to the successes of African-Caribbean women and their use of gender specific strategies (Fuller, 1982; Riley, 1986; Mac an Ghaill, 1988). The conclusions are that African-Caribbean women are more able to deal with the racism in the education system in the UK. Consequently they out-perform their male peers except at degree level studies (Jones, 1993). Furthermore, more African-Caribbean women than men are returning to education as mature students. According to data from the Labour Force Survey (Spring, 1994):

> More black young women (52%) were in full-time education than men (36%). Among other ethnic groups more young men than women were in full-time education. (Runnymede Bulletin, June 1995)

Male responses

Women have a high participation in African-Caribbean groups and organisations that are at the forefront of maintaining and rebuilding African cultural identities. However, humans are not passive and African-Caribbean men have been active in their responses to the pressures threatening to open up a chasm between themselves and their female colleagues. This is exemplified in four different reactive schemes aimed at African-Caribbean males: the Moyenda: Black Fathers Project, responses to school exclusions, mentor schemes, and the establishment of Leeds Black Men's Forum.

(1) Based in London, the Moyenda Black Fathers Project was a scheme of workshop discussions initiated by Exploring Parenthood. The project allowed African-Caribbean fathers the opportunity to discuss issues concerning the changing nature of their role as fathers. At the forefront of such debates is the added dimension of their ethnic experiences.

(2) In the 5-16 education system, school exclusion is used as a weapon against Black learners and, ultimately, the African-Caribbean community. This is especially significant for African-Caribbean boys. Educational activists, particularly in the London Borough of Lewisham, were so concerned about this growing

trend that as a counter-measure they initiated an action research project called the Positive Image Education Project. The project offers research development and practical advice and support to excluded schoolchildren and their parents/carers. In Leeds an organisation called Leeds Reach performs a similar function. Other Leeds complementary intervention youth schemes are organised by the Palace Youth Project and the Mandela Centre. Also of importance are the supplementary education programmes of the Afrikan Curriculum Development Association, Chapeltown Community Centre, Chapeltown and Harehills Assisted Learning Computer School, Chapeltown Independent After School, Chapeltown Young People's 10-2 Club, Marcus Garvey Media, and the Chapeltown and Harehills Area Motor Project.

(3) Mentor schemes are an attempt to rebuild self-esteem and confidence in African-Caribbean young people who in turn will be able to pass on their survival skills. Such advice and support schemes have been developed in cities such as Leeds, London and Nottingham. Hackney Council in London is considering a scheme that may *'introduce male role models into the classroom to work alongside the teacher. ... The CRE are working on a number of pilot schemes involving mentoring, including one with the Prince's Trust and another involving their own staff. They are also organising a symposium for the end of November [1995] to bring together various mentoring schemes'* (Amin, 1995). Mentoring now appears to be widely accepted as one means of tackling the alienation of some people in the African-Caribbean and South Asian communities.

(4) There have also been men's projects and meetings in Birmingham, Manchester, Nottingham and Sheffield. Other notable projects include the Ackee Project in Bradford, the African-Caribbean Men's Forum in Oxford (started in February 1997), Black Men's Groups in Huddersfield and Nottingham, Harlesden and Stonebridge Support Group in London and the Nubian Men's Group in Bradford. In this climate a key organisation called the Black Men's Forum emerged in Leeds from a day conference of one hundred men of African descent. The introduction to this book refers to the unique event entitled 'Black Men in Britain: March-

ing into the Millennium', that took place in 1997 at the West Yorkshire Playhouse in Leeds. The conference was initiated by Chapeltown and Harehills Enterprise Limited (Chel) Community Trust with financial aid from nine local voluntary and statutory organisations. In a pre-conference press release Clinton Cameron of Chel Community Trust stated that:

All men are affected by the massive changes that have been taking place in recent years in terms of employment, education and the effects on society. But some of these changes have particular implications for men of African descent. This is the first opportunity for Black men to meet as a group in Leeds to look at these issues and to work out how they will respond in the new millennium. (Hylton [ed.] 1997, 1)

The conference reviewed the position of men of African descent living in the UK with particular focus on men living in Leeds. Issues such as school exclusions, unemployment, petty crime and imprisonment, fatherhood responsibilities and the lack of male proactivity in community groups were discussed. In broad terms the conference aimed to raise the awareness of the challenges faced by individual men of African descent discuss methods of creating strong individuals, families and community, focus attention on positive alternatives to anti-social behaviour, challenge the negative disabling stereotypes and provide information about voluntary and statutory services that can support such goals.

The ideas dsicussed at this conference have moved the debate forward. There has to be an assessment of individual persona, an idea of what it means to be of African descent. Positive actions depend on a clear understanding of one's own immediate community (people of African descent) and the wider community (European). People of African descent have to make active and positive lifestyle choices that enhance themselves and their community, and men who have pride and self-respect can act as role models for others – as responsible parent, spouse or partner. Using Black self-help initiatives, respecting self and others and supporting creative people of African descent were identified as key strategies. The conference confirmed the survival methods by which men of African descent overcome their social exclusion from mainstream UK society. They know they need strength and commitment to create constructive actions rather than being sucked into survival strategies which do not enhance their self-esteem, family or community. For instance, one local speaker described the deciding moment when he faced this and began to channel his energies into a Self-Build housing co-operative. The key recommendations included:

• the implementation of practical schemes to reduce school exclusions of adolescent boys of African descent

• improvements in recruitment and training of men of African descent

• establishing 'grounding' or consciousness raising events for local African and African-Caribbean men

• strengthening the physical and communication networks between men of African descent in Leeds by creating an African Men's Forum and a newsletter

• encouraging the establishment of local independent financial saving schemes such as Pardoners and Credit Unions

• arranging meetings with representatives of Leeds City Council, Leeds Racial Equality Council and local training providers to discuss the implications of the conference.

To co-ordinate these recommendations the conference planning group reformed to become the Black Men's Forum, and their national conference in October 1998 for the first time brought together representatives of all local Black men's forums. As a national body, it aims to assist the creation of more local forums for men of African descent and to create the basis for a national co-ordinating committee of forum groups.

Summary outcome

Discussions on gender in both separate and integrated groups during the past five years, show clearly that female and male experiences are at the heart of being Black in inner-city UK, with its tensions around unemployment, racism, social exclusion and sexual roles. Many of the coping strategies adopted by African-Caribbean females are not accredited outside the African-Caribbean community, but women may nevertheless view their approach as a catalyst for African-Caribbean self-solution and continuation in the UK. Lone parents in Leeds express African-Caribbean consensus themes.

It's definitely the women who are at the forefront of change.

Lots of women, including myself, had low self esteem, but now they are going the other way and building up a foundation, and realising that I have got to do this on my own.

... you have to anyway you have no choice.

A lot of women are re-educating themselves, and finding their own self-worth (3 August 1993).

Males may also view their actions as safeguarding the cultural dignity of UK African-Caribbean values. The ongoing individual and community debates and negotiation create tensions between the gender groups. Approaches adopted by women may be regarded by some males as capitulating to a white racist society that does not respect them and perhaps as 'selling out'. Women may view their actions as a different form of resistance because they are fighting in a different manner. This different approach involves a critique of the actions of some young African-Caribbean males, although this may not produce a permanent female/male split. However, there are exceptions such as the upwardly mobile women described by Lesley Thomas (1995). Furthermore it is pre-supposed that the struggles for African-Caribbean survival and *umoja* (which means unity in Swahili) occur in the public sphere and thus neglect the private gender negotiations that might have a bearing on the choice of actions surfacing as public outcomes. Large numbers of women are actively involved in African-Caribbean groups and organisations that are at the forefront of maintaining and rebuilding an African cultural identity. According to a male education activist who is involved in several Leeds education and social organisations at management committee level:

The men is coming forward extremely slow, the young women of the Afro-Caribbean [community] are involving themselves in the structures and all organisations to a very full and greater degree. ... It is not the case for Afro-Caribbean male[s], you have actually got to screw them down to get them to put any commitment into any organisation, and it's something that I think the older members will have to work hard and try to pick them off one by one. (6 April 1995)

The involvement and importance of women in organisational activity were noted by socialist and activist Max Farrar in 1982. In an article analysing the 1981 street uprisings in Leeds he observed that:

> In Chapeltown, over the years, the backbone of community organising has been female, among blacks and whites. There were plenty of women on the streets during the uprising, and it is women who are central to the events after the violence: ... in Chapeltown, the prime movers of the Defence Committee are women.

He endorsed his remarks with a quote from *Spare Rib* of September 1981:

> Women, mainly black, (are) left to do the cleaning up afterwards; the women are the ones who face police harassment when the homes are searched; it's the women, the mums, who bear the brunt of the worry of finding the money to foot the bill for the kids fined by the court.
>
> Women are an integral part of the struggle – some of us are daughters, mothers, wives of those convicted, injured, imprisoned, and some have taken to the streets too.

African-Caribbean women are determined to build a strong Black female world to resist and challenge racism, and this is recognised by African-Caribbean men. As one – a community business advisor based in Leeds – frankly admitted:

> I get more satisfaction working with women because you find that women are a bit more on the ball these days, ... and when you advise them they take your advice and do things, and they get going. (20 April 1995)

Women employ contradictory or two-pronged approaches which entail rejecting some aspects of male responses to racism and social exclusion. This might include rejecting male tactics and male actors, although it may well be that they wish to challenge and change the male world so that male actions will be constructive. Rejection is seldom total because allegiances will still be made to combat the negativity of some aspects of the *'white world'* (3 August 1993). In this push for change and constructive support and for effective opposition to racism and social exclusion, the rise of UK Black men's forums is therefore welcomed and supported by women in their community.

So it appears that the ongoing gender debates in the African-Caribbean community and the building of Black men's forums form a key aspect of African-Caribbean community regeneration or re-

mobilisation. The actions of formal, informal, permanent and imper-
manent groupings such as the Association of Pan African Studies and
Initiatives in London, the Ackee Project in Bradford, the African-
Caribbean Men's Forum in Oxford, Black Men's Groups in Huddersfield and Nottingham, the Black Men's Forum in Leeds, the British
African-Caribbean Enterprise Club in London, Harlesden and Stonebridge Support Group, the Nubian Men's Group in Bradford,
Moyenda: Black Fathers Project in London, the West Indian Family
Counselling Service in Leeds, the United Male Forum in London, and
various community centre workers are geared to the creation of
forums where individual experiences can be expressed in a collective
manner. It is clearly understood that there are collective pressures
from external forces and from within the community. Individual
experiences resonate with collective experiences and consciousness.
The key solutions entail a sharing of collective pain, leading to
changed individual psychological and physical strategies which can, in
turn, lead to changed collective structures refocusing the lifestyles of
individuals, families, and the wider African-Caribbean community in
the UK.

The debates have an impact on actions taken in the private and public
spheres of activities and these feed back on each other. In the private
sphere there is concern about the risks for boys of falling behind
academically, being excluded from school, becoming involved in petty
crime and fears about their contact with the police and other sections
of the criminal justice system. This can be the vicious circle that cul-
minates in further exclusion from mainstream UK society and from
the support of African-Caribbean women when these boys become
adolescents and adults. The public sphere of activity offers various
intervention strategies organised by individuals and groups. In Leeds
these include the various youth schemes organised by the Palace
Youth Project, the Mandela Centre, the supplementary education programmes of the Afrikan Curriculum Development Association,
Chapeltown and Harehills Assisted Learning Computer School,
Chapeltown Independent After School, Chapeltown Young People's
10-2 Club, Marcus Garvey Media and the Chapeltown and Harehills
Area Motor Project. And in Lewisham a significant example of group
support for African-Caribbean male children, the Positive Image

Education Project, offers research development and practical advice and support to excluded schoolchildren and their parents/carers. Leeds Reach offers similar support.

Entering the public area in much the same way are issues relating to individual private interpersonal friendships between African-Caribbean women and men – the lack of trust, misunderstandings, and the rivalry over socio-economic position and job security. This is reflected in the increasing discussions and growing number of groups concerned with the creation of positive African identities and the sustenance of African and African-Caribbean gender relationships. As well as the public discussion themes and group discussions, there is a steady stream of Black publications. They are divided into several specific areas: some are self-help manuals to assist individuals in their quest for positive consciousness. Newspaper and journal articles and books provide insights into aspects of interpersonal gender friendships. There are also parenting courses for African-Caribbean individuals and couples, such as Exploring Parenthood Moyenda programmes, and research projects highlighting the changing nature of African-Caribbean individual, family and community regeneration. Published research in this area deals with stepfamily reformation (Hylton, 1995), the family role of men (Dench, 1996), maintaining and changing ethnic identities (Madood, Beishon and Virdee, 1994), coping strategies of African-Canadian and UK African-Caribbean men (Bernard, 1995) African and African-Caribbean family survival strategies (Hylton, 1997a) and the pending publication of research by Goulbourne, Chamberlain and Plaza: *Living Arrangements, Family Structure and Social Change of Caribbeans in Britain.*

The overall picture is of a pressurised yet dynamic community, privately and publicly trying to grapple individually and collectively with the changing nature of life in the UK.

Chapter 4
Conclusion

This book set out to examine a range of African-Caribbean community organisations in Leeds and London so as to explore the construction of individual and collective self-identity and reflective ideas. A wealth of qualitative data was generated to ascertain the reasons for the existence and continuance of these groups. A purposefully selected sample of eleven key activists offered in-depth analysis, not only describing the nature and extent of their activities in various community groups but also providing valuable insights about their reasons for becoming involved in group activity, their future hopes and fears.

African-Caribbean group actions are a reactive response to overt and covert racism and to the various forms of social exclusion faced in their daily lives in the UK. Where existing support services are inappropriate they have initiated their own cultural organisations. Group actions provide the individual with practical and emotional skills to overcome practical difficulties. Action begins the process of self-healing. All too often racism and forms of social exclusion from key provisions in UK society such as education, health care and employment, can leave people angry and confused to a degree that can generate and then sustain low self-esteem. African-Caribbean groups reverse this downward spiral by regenerating these clients to create a new positive individual and collective identity. Group formation is an aspect of group survival strategies and a way of restructuring aspects of community life to provide culturally specific services that are usually of a holistic nature. Whereas mainstream voluntary and statutory organisations treat clients as discrete beings isolated from their community and culture, African-Caribbean community groups are aware that clients have to deal with interlocking problems.

These groups are usually Africancentric. They use African names, African concepts and they question western Eurocentric ideas, actions and interpretations of history which exclude African knowledge. The Swahili word *Umoja* (unity) is a widely used African concept in these organisations. The linkage of African languages with the rebuilding of a positive African-Caribbean/African identity is widespread. Acquisition of an African language such as Swahili or Yoruba, or at least understanding and using key words and phases, is an important aspect of African-Caribbean community mobilisation.

African-Caribbean activists become involved in organisations to empower themselves and others. They work to create a new concept of their self-identity by redefining their ethnic group. Group actions are initiated as counter-actions to the effects of racism and social exclusion. There are certain barriers that affect the successful formation of African-Caribbean self-organised groups. These include age differentials; the problem of keeping control of group aims and objectives despite the wishes of funders; differences in organisational methods; gender divisions incorporating female success; and the difficulties associated with integrating new activists in an environment where groups are organised in a close spatial location such as the Chapeltown district of Leeds.

The creation of a group is linked to issues of survival. To choose to join a campaign or to ask for advice are choices of a specific type of survival strategy. Survival here begins with sharing pain and arriving at a notion of self-hood and self-reflection shaped with like-minded others who share similar pain and experiences, and who are hoping for similar solutions to the problems you all oppose. While there is ample evidence of the power of difference and the fight against discrimination and racism – outward actions – a major concern of African-Caribbeans is a critique of their private interactions with family and group members – inward actions. By introspection they examine their individual and collective ideas and behaviour while simultaneously they organise against racist attacks. Critique is positioned inward and outwards. Therefore, group action explanations which concentrate on the outward or external features of actions, will only connect with half the concerns of African-Caribbean actions. An example of this is class-based theories, which do not concentrate on the private areas of action. Whereas theories that focus on public and private aspects of actions, can promote a greater understanding about African-Caribbean ideas, aspirations and behaviour patterns. Such holistic theories include Africancentric concerns, critical theory and post-modernism paradigms.

Defining self is a difficult process. It changes over time and is subject to many influences. But how does an individual maintain a positive self-image? Only through a deep understanding of self can individuals hope to make sense of their place in their families and their communities, and so assess their presence and roles in relation to other individuals, other families and other visual minority groups. All such self-analyses and interpersonal and group negotiations have to be achieved against a background of negatives designed to confuse and destroy any sense of well-being. The individual response to these issues has to be focused on ideas and actions that do not destroy self or others. The struggle is about not hating one's self and – equally important – not hating others. In the building of these dual positives, sub-groups of a religious and cultural nature such as Rastafarians and other Africancentric believers have an excellent track record.

African-Caribbean group actions do not carry a notion of pay-back. A more correct analogy would be having a shield or erecting a barrier behind which to shelter. They may be psychologically and physically hurt behind the barrier but they remain alive. Behind the barrier they can repair their psychological and physical wounds by trying to understand their true selves. They can then go forward – not to attack others but forward in the sense of acquiring new hopes and strategies that will allow the negatives to bounce off their psyche so they can survive without falling under the impact. Yet this new-found sense of power can become intimidating to those who fired the negative punches, because to throw a punch is to hope it connects and hurts. If the negatives and potential harm are circumvented, if African-Caribbeans can reflect back the negatives to their opponents, then this strategy has the potential to cause confusion. Thus the building of individual self-confidence and self-knowledge is one of the key functions of group formation and actions.

Unsurprisingly, the issue African-Caribbeans articulate as most determining their reactive group actions is their exclusion from UK society. They are concerned about practical and emotional rejection. The practical rejection focuses on the many areas of their lives where discrimination occurs either as explicit denial, access and usage of particular services such as housing, education, social services or counselling or as implicit denial, for instance being channelled into specific occupational and recreational areas such as sport and music. Such channelling is one form of social exclusion because other areas of recreating self-hood are effectively closed off or have *de facto* restricted entry.

Group actions are counter-measures not only for building new structures but for upholding theoretical precedents concerned with equality of service and access. Without self-organised groups, African-Caribbeans could become easy targets or victims. Group actions, although mainly reactive, are productive by the very action of group formation, so that potential victims act in their own interests by becoming actors and combatants. This implies a sense of separateness incorporating separate actions based on feelings of a shared culture, ethnicity, pain and history.

African-Caribbeans operate a double strategy, building alternative emotional and practical individual and group support systems while also making efforts to change existing voluntary and statutory service provisions so they understand their concerns better (Goulbourne, 1988). The hope is that support organisations will change and cater for their needs. For African-Caribbeans to rely solely on this possibility is to court disaster and disappointment, and the activists encountered in this research did not make this mistake. One of the key aspects of African-Caribbean self-organisation is to discuss and create a notion of self-belief and an individual and collective understanding about themselves. Only when individuals have appropriated a style of knowledge satisfying their inner self-hood are they able to put forward demands to mainstream service providers, central and local government departments and Eurocentric voluntary organisations to change their existing services. At the same time they may also be constructing alternative individual and communal arrangements supporting their needs and fulfilling their practical and emotional requirements as African/Caribbean people.

As has been shown, African-Caribbeans require a true concept of their self-identity as a shield against the negative practical and emotional assaults to their physical and psychological survival in the UK. But this shield cannot be solely prescribed by public policy provisions. While public policy provisions may be necessary, their impact forms only a small part of the survival mechanisms assisting African-Caribbeans to feel whole. Positive self-consciousness, the elucidation of African and African-Caribbean history and culture have to be sought, discussed and then internalised. Only then can these have a positive effect on the manner in which they construct and reconstruct their lives in both private and public spheres. African-Caribbean community activities help to sustain and perform key functions of recreating and sustaining African-Caribbean individual and group identity. This is one of the reasons why the aims, objectives and working methods of the groups is so fiercely defended. The essence of the overall data from African-Caribbean activists suggests that this defence and the sense of independence of ideas and activity are historically significant, harking back to colonialism and the reduction of self-direction during the period of transatlantic slavery. Perceived loss of autonomy by diasporian Africans, whether practical or emotional, will invariably conjure up a past that African-Caribbeans are determined will not return.

Theorists of African decent such as Asante (1992), hooks (1991), Biko (in Woods, 1978) and Fanon (1965) are in agreement that the loss of methods of constructing a positive concept of self or a positive African consciousness is as grave as the loss of physical freedom. A positive view of self may even be more important than physical freedom. If you free your mind the freedom of the body will follow. These activists and theorists know that while Africans in the diaspora may be physically free, their minds may be lost. Individuals could still be enslaved – what Bob Marley termed 'mental slavery', where 'none but we can free up our mind'. True freedom requires finding one's true self or inner consciousness, because only then can positive survival strategies be constructed which can act as a shield against physical and psychological negatives directed against self and community.

Barriers to group formations

This book documents the extent of the barriers individuals have to overcome in order to establish African-Caribbean group actions. The main external barriers to African-Caribbean group formation are racism and various forms of social exclusion, and the main internal barriers are (a) age differentials, (b) the control of group aims, (c) gender divisions and (d) parochial behaviour. These issues are summarised below.

(a) Unsurprisingly, African-Caribbeans born in the UK tend to organise in a different manner from the older community members who were born in the Caribbean. This is due partly to the nature of the racism heaped upon young African-Caribbean people. It mainly concerns education or the lack of it, unemployment, involvement in the criminal justice system and diagnosis and mis-treatment in mainstream mental health provision. These negative pressures have had profound effects on young African-Caribbean men and they are more difficult than African-Caribbean young women to draw into or keep involved in group activities. And there are other intervening variables related to gender division issues discussed below.

(b) Controlling the type of organisation that is formed is a vital issue in African-Caribbean group activity. There are questions about how the group is to be formed, who is involved in the formation, what type of services are performed and for whom. It is not just a matter of funding, although this is important, especially where groups devise schemes to reduce the control of the funders. Autonomy is important because unless the group actions are the correct ones, chosen by African-Caribbeans and carried out by African-Caribbeans, they become tokenistic. Lost of autonomy is usually associated with paternalism and has echoes of trans-atlantic slavery. Autonomy or self-control is about self-activity. African-Caribbean activists organise actions by and for themselves. It is action from below, or changing the self by one's own deeds. This approach to problem solving is based on the notion that individuals are aware of their problems and should therefore be equipped to change the situation. If individuals do not have the skills to make these changes they should be able to appoint others who do not reduce their agency. Action becomes our action. Changes to individual self-confidence and the creation of group identity show that it is we who did it.

(c) We have seen that it is difficult to recruit young African-Caribbean men to group action, and that African-Caribbean women use the education system to better effect. Alongside this public gender division, African-Caribbean women have demanded changed conditions in their interpersonal relationships with African-Caribbean men, most notably mutual respect and emotional support. These demands are exacerbated by the effects of racism and social exclusion that tend to push the men more to the margins of UK society. The variables threaten to open up a chasm between women and men, making it more difficult for them to co-operate in personal matters and in the public sphere such as when creating group actions. The tensions between the sexes are ever present because they are linked to unresolved issues.

(d) There is an African-Caribbean focus on changing the self through the medium of group actions. Operating as a lone individual is thus rejected. Racism affects the individual but that individual is singled out from a negatively labelled group – and any group member can be singled out. African-Caribbeans are aware of the mechanisms involved in the various forms of social exclusion and their response is to fight back as a group – a response that is easier if its members trust each other. Past events have shown that African-Caribbeans can react quickly to racist situations by arranging public meetings and forming defensive organisations. In Leeds such speedy responses occur because people of African descent are located in defined areas where activists know each other and can respond quickly to attacks aimed on individuals or the group. Africans or African-Caribbeans newly arrived in Leeds tend to have to serve an apprenticeship period before their ideas and actions are accepted, and this is intensified if the outsider tries to assume leadership of a group. The barrier is a mechanism for protecting the known spatial group from potential failure. Sharing the same ethnicity does not provide the individual with an automatic right to involvement in group actions.

We all live close to the edge. There is a thin line between being strong and psychologically and physically healthy, with a positive sense of self, and mental and physical deterioration and breakdown. Like a moth hovering close to a naked flame, we can be drawn into the flame and be hurt or killed. The question is, how can people remain in the joy of the light without destroying themselves? The answer appears to be that If their sense of individual identity is reinforced by everyday structures and provisions such as education, arts, the media and mainstream advice and information networks, they are able to overcome the negative whenever it arises. African-Caribbeans face a scenario where these everyday structures seldom reinforce their positive sense of self-hood. The only sources of affirmation may be friends, family members and community groups – although they too, face much the same pressures. There are two possible outcomes: either family and friends prove unable to provide support because they are undermined by similar negatives and pressures as the person seeking support, or these family, friends and other community group members can offer understanding and support precisely because they experience the same pressures but do not internalise the pain. As Bob Marley said: *'who feels it, knows it'*.

Bibliography

Ackah, W. and Christian, M. (eds.) (1997) *Black Organisation and Identity in Liverpool: A Local, National and Global Perspective*, Liverpool, Charles Wootton College Press

Agustus, P. (1994) *Baby Father*, New Jersey, X Press

Ani, M. (1994) *Yurugu*, New Jersey, African World Press

Asante, M. K. (1992) *Kemet, Afrocentricity and Knowledge*, New Jersey, African World Press

Asante, M. K. (1988) *Afrocentricity*, New Jersey, African World Press

Bacal, A. (1991) *Ethnicity in the Social Sciences – A view and review of the literature on ethnicity*, Coventry, Paper in Ethnic Relations No 3, Centre for Research in Ethnic Relations, University of Warwick

Baptise, A. (1994) *Single Black Female*, London, X Press

Bones, J. (1985) *One Love, Rastafari: History, Doctrine and Livity*, London, Voice of Rasta

Bourne, J. Bridges, L. and Seale, C. (1994) *Outcast England: How Schools Exclude Black Children*, London, Institute of Race Relations

Browder, A. T. (1989) *From the Browder File*, Washington D. C. The Institute of Karmic Guidance

Butterworth, E. (ed.) (1967) *Immigrants in West Yorkshire: Social Conditions and the Lives of Pakistanis, Indians, and West Indians*, London, Institute of Race Relations

Castells, M. (1983) *The City and the Grassroots*, London, Edward Arnold

Dench, G. (1996) *The Place of Men in Changing Family Cultures*, London, Institute of Community Studies

Dench, G. (1975) *Maltese in London*, London, Routledge and Kegan Paul

Dennis, F. (1988) *Behind The Frontlines*, London, Gollancz

Diop, C. A. (1991) *Civilization or Barbarism*, New York, Lawrence Hill Books

Diop, C. A. (1974) *The African Origin of Civilization*, New York, Lawrence Hill Books

Fanon, F. (1986) *Black Skin White Mask*, (translated by C. L. Markmann) London, Pluto

Fanon, F. (1965) *The Wretched of the Earth*, London, Macgibbon and Kee

Fryer, P. (1991) *Staying Power*, London, Pluto

Gillborn, D. and Gipps, C. (1996) *Recent research on the achievements of ethnic minority pupils*, London, HMSO.

Gilroy, P. (1993) *The Black Atlantic*, London, Verso

Gilroy, P. (1987) *There Ain't no Black in the Union Jack*, London, Hutchinson

Goulbourne, H. (ed.) (1990) *Black Politics in Britain*, Research in Ethnic Relations Series, Aldershot, Avebury

Goulbourne, H. (1988) *West Indian Political Leadership in Britain*, The Byfield Memorial Lecture 1987, Coventry, Centre for Research in Ethnic Relations, University of Warwick, Occasional Paper No. 4

Gramsci, A. (1987) Hoare, Q. and Smith, E. (ed.) *Gramsci – Selections from the Prison Notebooks*, London, Lawrence and Wishart

Hannerz, U. (1969) *Soulside: Inquiries into Ghetto Culture and Community*, New York, Columbia University Press

Haynes, A. (1996) *This is where I live*, London, Runnymede Trust

hooks, b. (1991) *Yearning race, gender and cultural politics*, London, Turnaround

Hylton, C. (ed.) (1997) *Black Men in Britain: Marching into the Millennium*, Leeds, Bogle-L'Ouverture and the Black Men's Forum

Hylton, C. (1997a) *Family Survival Strategies: Moyenda Black Families Talking*, London, Exploring Parenthood

Hylton, C. (1995) *Coping With Change: Family Transitions in Multi-Cultural Communities*, London, National Stepfamily Association

James, G. G. M. (1992) *Stolen Legacy*, New Jersey, African World Press

Jones, D. (1993) *Culture Bandits 2*, Philadelphia, Hikeka Press

Jones, T. (1993) *Britains Ethnic Minorities*, London, Policy Studies Institute

Koestler, A. (1968) *The Sleepwalkers*, New York, Macmillan

Koval, J. (1988) *White Racism*, New York, Free Association Press

Law, I. Hylton, C. Karmani, A. and Deacon, A. (1994) Racial Equality and Social Security Service Delivery: A study of the perceptions and experiences of black minority ethnic people eligible for benefit in Leeds, *Sociology and Social Policy Research Working Paper 10*, Leeds, University of Leeds

Mac an Ghaill, M. (1988) *Young, Gifted and Black*, Milton Keynes, Open University Press

Madood, T. Beishon, S. and Virdee, S. (1994) *Changing Ethnic Identities*, London, Policy Studies Institute

Majors, R. and Billson J. M. (1992) *Cool Pose: The Dilemmas of Black Manhood in America*, New York, Simon and Schuster

Mandel, E. (1977) *From Class Society to Communism: An Introduction to Marxism*, London, Ink Links

Mann, M. (1973) *Consciousness and Action Among the Western Working Class*, London, Macmillan

Marcuse, H. (1972) *Counter Revolution and Revolt*, London, Allen Lane

Melucci, A. (1989) *Nomads of the Present: Social Movements and Individual needs in Contemporary Society*, (Keane, J. and Mier, P. eds.) London, Hutchinson Radius

Moore, B. Jr. (1974) *Social Origins of Dictatorship and Democracy*, London, Penguin University Books

Parkin, F. (1971) *Class Inequality and Political Order: Social Stratification in Capitalist and Communist Societies*, London, Granada

Priestley, M. (1998) *Disability Politics and Community Care*, London, Jessica Kingsley Publications Limited

Ramdin, R. (1987) *The Making of the Black Working Class in Britain*, Aldershot, Gower

Rex, J. (1991) *Ethnic Identity and Ethnic Mobilisation in Britain*, Coventry, Centre for Research in Ethnic Relations, University of Warwick

Rex, J. (1983) *Race Relations in Sociological Theory*, London, Routledge and Kegan Paul

Robins, D. (1992) *Tarnished Visions*, Oxford, Oxford University Press

Scott, J. C. (1985) *Weapons of the Weak*, Yale, Yale University Press

Scott, J. C. (1976) *The Moral Economy of the Peasants*, Yale, Yale University Press

Sewell, T. (1987) *Garvey's Children*, London, Voice Communications

Sivanandan, A. (1990) *Communities of Resistance: writings on Black struggles for socialism*, London, Verso

Werbner, P. and Anwar, M. (eds.) (1991) *Black and Ethnic Leaderships in Britain, The cultural dimensions of political action*, London, Routledge

Woods, D. (1978) *Biko*, London, Paddington Press

Articles

Farrar, M. (1993) 'Racism, Education and Black Self-Organisation', in *Critical Social Policy*, 36

Farrar, M. (1988) 'The Politics of Black Youth Workers in Leeds', in *Critical Social Policy*, 23

Farrar, M. (1982) 'Riot and Revolution: the politics of an inner city', in *Big Flame*, 8

Fuller, M. (1982) 'Young female and black', in Cashmore, E. and Troyna, B. (eds.) *Black Youth in Crisis*, London, Allen and Unwin

Goulbourne, H. (1993) 'Aspects of Nationalism and Black Identities in Post-Imperial Britain', in Cross, M. and Keith, M. (eds.) *Racism, the City and the State*, London, Routledge

Hylton, C. Blake, V. Auber, P. Kasule, S. Karisa, L. and Kopoka, T. (1996) 'Afrikan and Afrikan-Caribbean education: the case of Leeds based Afrikan Curriculum Development Association', in Barrett, E. and Ewart, B. (eds.) *Voices from the Grassroots*, Leeds, Department of Adult Continuing Education, University of Leeds

Jamerson, F. (1985) 'Postmodernism and Consumer Society', in Foster, H. (ed.) *Postmodern Culture*, London, Pluto

Jamerson, F. (1984) 'Postmodernism or the Cultural Logic of Late Capitalism', *New Left Review*, 146

James-Fergus, S. (1997) 'Rebuilding the African-Caribbean in Britain', in Dench, G. (ed.) *Rewriting the sexual contract*, London, Institute of Community Studies

Kant, E. (1973) 'Groundwork', in Wolf, R. *The Autonomy of Reason*, London, Harper Row

McLennan, G. (1990) 'The Power of Ideology', in Unit 17, D103 *Society and Social Science: A Foundation Course*, Block IV, Milton Keynes, Open University Press

Melucci, A. (1988) 'Getting Involved: Identity and Mobilization in Social Movements', in Klandermans, B. Kriesi, H. and Tarrow, S. (eds.) *Internal Social Movement Research*, Vol 1, JAI Press

Riley, K. (1986) 'Black girls speak for themselves', in Weiner, G. (ed.) *Just a Bunch of Girls*, Milton Keynes, Open University Press

Wann, M. (1995) *The development of self help activities*, York, Joseph Rowntree Foundation, Social Care Summary 5

Wolf, R. E. (1987) 'On Peasant Rebellions', in Shanin, T. (ed.) *Peasants and Peasant Societies*, Oxford, Basil Blackwell

Wolf, R. E. (1969) 'Peasant Wars of the Twentieth Century', in Paige, J. M. (ed.) (1975) *Agrarian Revolution: Social Movements and Export Agriculture in the Underdeveloped World*, London, Macmillan

Newspapers and magazines

The Alarm, (September-October 1996) No 20, London, Alarm Promotions

The Alarm, (November 1995) No 15, London, Alarm Promotions

Alibhai-Brown, Y. (13 June 1994) 'Call me Daddy', *Guardian*

Amin, K. (September 1995) 'Parents and Role Models: Two Projects', London, *Runnymede Bulletin*

Black Direct Action, (November 1994) Newsletter No 1, Leeds

Chapeltown News, (July, August, October, November 1993) Leeds

Diaspora, (March 1994) No 1, London

Ford, R. (21 July 1993) 'Fathers 'touch down' – and flee', *The Times*

Maroon, (May-June 1996), No 1, Vol 1, Leeds

Ouseley, H. (2 July 1993) 'Young, single and black', *The Independent*

Runnymede Bulletin, (June 1995)

Taylor, S. (November 1992) 'Affirming Our Men', *Essence*, No 59, USA

Thomas, L. (19 February 1995) 'She's gotta have it all', *Sunday Times*

Other documents
Department of Education, (1992)
Simba conference leaflet, (August 1996) London
United Male Forum leaflet, (1994) London

Unpublished documents
Bernard, W. (1995) *Working with men for change*, Unpublished PhD, University of Sheffield

Goulbourne, H. Chamberlain, M. and Plaza, D. (1995) *Living Arrangements, Family Structure and Social Change of Caribbeans in Britain*, Research Outline, Cheltenham and Gloucester College of Higher Education

Hylton, C. (1997) *African-Caribbean Community Self Organisations: A Leeds Case Study*, Department of Sociology and Social Policy, University of Leeds, PhD, October 1997

Wieviorka, M. (1992) *Ethnicity as Action*, Ethnic Mobilisation in Europe in the 1990s Conference Paper, Warwick University